DOING THI

ONE
Thing
WILL

CHANGE YOUR LIFE
FOREVER!

The Self Help Guide to Personal
Growth & Healthy Relationships

Jacqui Olliver

EDUCATE PUBLISHING
NEW ZEALAND

Educate Publishing
www.educatepublishing.com
support@educatepublishing.com

Licensing options are available for schools and libraries. Special discounts available on quantity purchases by cor-porations, associations, and others. For details, contact the "Special Sales" at the email address above.

Doing This ONE Thing Will Change Your Life Forever!
by Jacqui Olliver

ISBN 978-0-473-41443-6 (Paperback)
ISBN 978-0-473-41444-3 (ePub)
ISBN 978-0-473-41445-0 (Mobi)
ISBN 978-0-473-41448-1 (eAudiobook)

Edited by Paul (Tiger) Diamond
Book cover by Adrienne Foote
Book Layout ©2017 BookDesignTemplates.com

Disclaimer: The insights featured in this book are the re-sult of the authors own research and discovery, written in layman's terms for easy understanding. Additional insights are on the author's website www.EndTheProblem.com

A catalog record for this book is available from the Na-tional Library of New Zealand: https://goo.gl/tha8vT

Contents

Part 1

Part 2

Dedication
This book is dedicated to all the people who have
touched my life and made me a better person.

"You are really amazing. Your views about human psychology and emotions will one day, change whole of medicine."

"Jacqui offers a readable, useful and important book. Jacqui is an intuitive counsellor, unusually intuitive to the point of gifted, and innovative and inventive enough to experiment far beyond the confines of academe, and emerge with a simple, clear counselling technology beyond mindfulness, or mere resilience training."

FOREWORD
PAUL (TIGER) DIAMOND

I descended from a long line of Tohunga (native teachers, mentors) and through my naturally enquiring mind I opened many Pandora boxes to find out how the modules complemented the "thing" in its entirety. I've been employed as a shooter, top salesman, snooker champion, artist, hypnotist, gang leader, extrusion foreman, engine builder, biker, cyclist, driver etc. From all these callings, I accrued a wide range of skills which allowed me to have a unique insight into many topics from which I conceptualized the Switching Technique. When I was at primary school my teachers wanted to advance me ahead four years, so my mother said.

When I first met Jacqui Olliver, it was to share a house. I enquired and was informed of her line of work. I had absolute unique information on her topic which was never before shared which I happily mentored her with, including the switching technique. She transformed from being an obscure national personality to a World-Renowned Practitioner sought by many clients worldwide for her "real answers" style of therapy which is totally unique from mainstream systems.

Jacqui's devotion to helping others overcome sexual and emotional problems stems from the impediments she encountered navigating her way through life. She has personally experienced many stumbling blocks on her way to solving the wider problems concerning personal growth, love and connection. I have seen her growth and this book reflects a candid and transparent view into her life. Reading this book will help unravel many mysteries and transform many lives.

INTRODUCTION

Have you ever wondered why it's such a challenge being human? Unlike a car, we didn't come with a guide which explains how to drive our body. We didn't have our emotions explained to us in a manner which enabled us to use them as a springboard to feel fantastic. Instead, we are totally overwhelmed to the point we just want to give up or bury our head in the sand.

The main impediment being, we didn't inherit the most basic skills to enhance living! It's small wonder so many people feel depressed, disconnected and alone. Anxiety and other strong emotions are often the reason why we are unable to solve bigger issues. As I eventually discovered from my own life experience, emotional problems generally result from lacking skills and knowledge, especially about the driving forces in our life.

Using real life examples, I explore and explain the reasons why emotions prevent us from not rectifying and resolving these issues. I've endeavored for this book to be a life "guide" which highlights what we need to know and the ultimate explanation of how to incorporate this feel good formula into everyday living. I'll show you how to neutralize any strong emotion within seconds and how to successfully navigate through the most complex challenges we all face in life.

Within these inspiring and motivating pages, you will find the answers to solving specific life situations. So, instead of being overwhelmed and feeling paralyzed by your fears, you can feel confident in moving forward and taking actionable steps to end your problems.

Doing this ONE thing will enhance how you take control of your life and make you feel more confident.

PART 1

Insights Gained from My Life Experiences

It seemed that I had been thrust into a turbulent life? After 11 hours of intense labor, I was eventually born at 3:40 am on the 23rd of July 1970, almost three weeks overdue and with my mother's belly so huge she could hardly fit in the back seat of the car which took her to the hospital.

Right from the outset I was constantly hungry to be fed. My mother had milk fever when my older sister was a baby. When it came time to feed me, her nipples quickly became cracked and sore which made it too painful for her to breast feed me. However, when given the substitute of cow's milk formula I started having some weird kind of shaking fits like convulsive full body tremors.

Confused, my mother took me to her doctor who was also confused as to what was causing the problem. He then referred us to a leading pediatrician who determined I had an allergy to cow's milk. She recommended a variety of alternate milks for us to try and as a family we all endured many sleepless nights until we found one which I could tolerate.

While determining which form of nourishment I could tolerate the pediatrician told Mum to lie me on my back and just watch me whenever I was having a fit. They were mild fits and she said that I would be safe on my back as long as I was being watched. When my father's mum came to visit, Mum vividly recalls her commenting with shock and consternation when Mum just laid me on the floor wrapped in my blanket when I started having one of these fits. I finally shook myself back into reality. Apparently for me in my first few months of life this was a normal procedure.

After months of incessant crying and an aversion to everything they tried to feed me, my parents desperate for rest and at the end of their tether finally found that I could tolerate soy milk. Finally, a reprieve! Without the constant pain and discomfort of different milk allergies I became a normal, happy and gurgling baby.

Until they tried to put me down to bed. My parents would spend hours taking it in turn trying to put me to bed, but I would cry as soon as I sensed them leave the room. It was as though I had radar and was born afraid to be left alone. I was not a naturally contented baby. Problems going to sleep and staying asleep tormented me throughout my early childhood. As I collated the insights for this chapter, my mother described me as "you were such a problem child."

I was two when I was encouraged into my own bed in my own bedroom. I would wake up in the middle of the night and take forever to go back to sleep. I was terrified of the monsters hiding under my bed and would lie rigidly in the middle of my bed, so they couldn't reach me. When I finally called out for help Mum would come in and sit on the edge of my bed with her feet on the floor to prove that it was safe. And then when she thought I had fallen asleep she would stand up and gingerly take one step

3

at a time, hoping to reach the door unnoticed. But as soon as she made it to the door I would wake up. It would usually take another hour or two of repeating this process until I eventually went back to sleep and she escaped.

Then I was given Rupert. He was a wind-up bear who would soothe my insecurities with a gentle, rhythmic tune as I cuddled up to him. Rupert lay in between me and the monsters, he was my protector. Being aware of the sensations of Rupert's fake fur against my body was oddly reassuring and comforting. Even to this day I easily remember that tune and the feelings of peaceful connection that his memory brings.

It's interesting to note that emotional responses to life are constantly changing – but under the age of two years old, emotional responses are an uncalculated part of life and rarely bothered us because of our younger age factor. Up until then we felt intensely alive and present in each moment, free from any thoughts of responsibility!

Every moment was exciting, and we were constantly reacting to whatever was in front of us. We would laugh, scream, shriek, giggle or squawk – we never judged what we were feeling, we simply experienced and participated in life as it presented itself. We were intensely alive; alert and vibrant.

At that young age, we had no knowledge of a past to judge ourselves against. Nor did we have the mental capacity at that time to analyze our thoughts or to think or worry about the future. We simply experienced life, moment by moment. We didn't hold on to thoughts of resentment. If we were hurt or afraid we would scream with shock, then cry and get over that strong emotion, usually within seconds.

Then we hit two years old; described by many adults as "the Terrible Two's." Why is it called that? Because that's when most kids begin verbalizing those intense emotions we call anger, frustration and fear.

When we were a baby we didn't have to think for ourselves. Feeding, changing clothes, our bed being uncomfortable, too hot, too cold, tired, hungry, we would simply cry or scream to have our demands met. At that stage in our life there were no expectations for us other than to grow and be healthy.

Whereas a two-year-old has gained a somewhat limited vocabulary as well as several decibels worth of vocal intensity! As a toddler, we try to ask for what we want and become loudly frustrated trying to understand why our request was being rejected. This, triggers verbal bouts of discomfort, resistance and other intense emotional responses to others within hearing range.

However, once we become capable of speaking, we're expected to stop acting like a baby and start communicating clearly. Yet, we're still too young to have the mental capacity to clearly communicate our wants and desires. This is why when we feel unheard, we put everything we've got into a muddled combination of whining, screaming and wild gesticulations in an attempt to feel heard and to have this particular need met.

But our parents are also having growing expectations of how we should be behaving. Yet, due to our lack of advanced communication skills, when we were small children and threw a tantrum in public we were often shut down and told to be quiet. We would be told to behave or that we would miss out on a treat or we would be cuddled and pacified. This was usually in an attempt to calm our parents down or in order to not offend other adults in the immediate vicinity!

How many times have you seen a parent and child at a shopping mall with the child screaming their demands at the top of their lungs? And the parent trying to pacify the child – or bribe them to be quiet? It's painful to watch.

Does this approach help to prepare the child to be an emotionally balanced and happy individual?

No, the parent is just buying themselves some time before the next inevitable emotional outburst! And they're inadvertently teaching their child to be dependent on using emotion in a negative way to get what they want in future. That's going to cause a LOT of grief and stress in the future of everyone involved.

Anger is an interesting emotion to experience as a young child. It's intense and fiery – but over quickly if we are left to deal with it ourselves (it's always the attention received by a child which fuels an ongoing emotional response.)

Obviously if a child is hungry, thirsty or tired they're going to be cranky. Make sure you take care of those basic needs of hunger, thirst, toiletry and entertainment before expecting a child to behave in public.

Because when we're young children we're too young to process a great deal of thought and we haven't gained the ability to assess the bigger picture. However, we do still have the in-built program of switching to the intense physical discomfort associated with an emotional response (such as frustration or anger) which allows that program to complete within seconds.

The Unique Logic of Children

From my young perspective, I believed I had started school at a disadvantage. There was a girl named Kristen whom I had attended Kindergarten with. I remember one day at kindergarten she pushed past me in the playground to get to the slide first. Feeling humiliated and self-righteous I decided in that moment that I didn't like her even though it was something that I would frequently do myself!

I was devastated on my first day of school when I was led into the classroom and there she was, smiling at me in triumph that she was obviously older than me as out of the two of us, she had started school first.

Kristen and I were both fast learners and highly competitive in all activities, both intellectually and physically outside in the playground.

Within the first couple of years of primary school, Kristen and I had grown to be such arch rivals until one day we were unexpectedly thrown together and our teacher firmly told us to collaborate on a particular project. We both loudly and indignantly resisted to no avail! Then Kristen looked contemptuously at me and stated, "You should be nice to me, it's my birthday tomorrow." I looked at her in shock and said, "And it's my birthday three days after then! You're only three days older than me!" And with the unique logic that only children possess, a strong friendship was forged in that moment.

In my early years at school I felt compelled to do better and learn faster than everyone else. Even though I had a great thirst for knowledge and to grow up, I was also desperately trying to garner my father's attention and gain his praise which were sadly absent in my life.

Personally, I LIVED to receive gold star stickers. There was an award board prominently displayed on every classroom wall which contained various subjects as well as our preferred behavior. Out of classes of about 30 kids, I was devastated if I didn't see my name and a gold star sticker up on that board every week.

My competitive nature sometimes kept me isolated from integrating with other children because I was constantly trying to prove myself instead of simply allowing myself to naturally fit in.

I was an adventurous child and I resisted the fact that my mother would send me to school dressed in frilly dresses. I would wear shorts and my favorite t-shirt underneath, so I could change as soon as I got to school and feel less encumbered when climbing trees and swinging my way across the playground. I grew up in a neighborhood full of boys and therefore grew up competitive, constantly proving that even as a girl, I was better, faster and stronger than all the boys.

It was SO embarrassing at school one day when I was happily swinging from a branch and heard those dreaded words, "Jacqueline Jean Olliver, you better come home RIGHT NOW!" Uh-oh. The use of my full name indicated that I was in a whole bunch of trouble. Unfortunately, my house overlooked the school and Mum just happened to glance out the window and saw me hanging from that branch in my shorts and t-shirt. I was humiliated that I had been caught out, other kids were looking at me and sniggering and I was totally devastated when Mum made me change back into the horrible frilly dress which I hated so much before sending me back to school.

I was always trying to be my own authority and live life how I wanted to. But as I grew up there were so many rules instilled in me for being a kid and my somewhat boisterous way of communicating my need for fun and independence seemed to fall on deaf ears as it didn't fit in with that adult's expectations of me.

It was different when I was a younger kid. Before I went to school I had total confidence in myself. However, I was surrounded by well-meaning adults who would inform me, "You can't do this... and you can't do that..." and little by little my confidence wavered. I started losing belief in myself.

Then there was Mrs Malone. She's the teacher who told me off for wanting to play on the grass field when it was closed due to raining the previous few hours. There were too many kids on the concreted area of the playground and it felt uncomfortably restricted. I didn't care if the grass was wet, there was more room for me to run around and feel like I was free. When I communicated my annoyance and frustration to her, she said, "Don't you get angry with me Jacqui Olliver you can't just do whatever you want, whenever you want to do it."

Comments like those from adults can have a devastating effect on children and most adults don't even realize it. When you're told often enough that you can't partic-

ipate in life how you want to, you can start losing your excitement for life, your sense of self-worth can diminish and the self-confidence required to go after what you want, and need can dissipate. And this all starts with a throwaway comment which is then fueled by a growing sense of separation.

In all those years spent at school in and out of the classroom, we were prevented from experiencing our intense emotions in the moment they were triggered. Instead, we were taught to be quiet and suppress our feelings. Not allowed to be angry. Not allowed to feel frustrated. Not allowed to be upset. Not allowed to make noise. We just weren't allowed to be anything other than obedient students.

Even when we expressed joyful emotions in the classroom, we were interrupted from experiencing them - and told to save them until lunchtime. This taught us to delay our emotional feelings and become trapped in the endless chatter and busyness of our mind. When we stop ourselves from feeling an emotional response we often default back to thinking about it as an unresolved issue.

It was around about this time that I started judging my responses to life – and therefore began a long journey into making myself feel isolated and alone. Ask a child what they want from life and they only want to be happy. Ask any adult the same question and they all want to feel better than they do now...

I remember being about 6 years old and being banished to my room for misbehaving. Mum firmly shut my bedroom door behind me and left me to it. I cried loudly for a while, hoping for some attention. Then I gave up after a few minutes when I realized I wasn't going to get any. I remember at that time feeling a wave of disappointment wash over me then switching my attention to getting my pencils out and happily coloring in a picture.

My mother was amazing in this way, she allowed me to experience my emotional responses but didn't encourage me to overindulge in them. She also didn't leave me hanging there for too long by myself. After about 15 minutes she'd knock on my door, poke her head in and suggest that if I was over my emotional outburst I might want to come and join her in doing a puzzle.

If we were lucky enough to experience this type of reprieve at home, we lost it when we went to school. Everything at school was regimented to a timetable so there were no exceptions!

Over the years we trained ourselves to suppress our anger and other intense emotions by trying to make them go away in the hope that we would become more acceptable to the adults around us. While this appeared to make the adults less hotwired by our behavior, it did nothing but detract from our own senses of self-confidence, self-worth and self-esteem.

The Consequences of Jumping to Conclusions

Then there was the year I nearly drowned. Mum, Dad and my sister Tania and I were visiting friends from our previous neighborhood. Tania and I were stoked because they had a pool for us kids to play in. Never having been taught how to swim we still both enjoyed being in the water.

Because we didn't know how to swim, the other girl modified a game of tag for us. We would chase each other around the inside edge of the pool, holding on to the concrete tiles surrounding the pool while we were inside it. Around and around we went, laughing breathlessly as we tried to stay in front of whomever was chasing us.

As I was looking behind me to see how close my chaser was I miscalculated where the edge of the pool was. My hand reached out and grabbed a handful of emptiness. Eeek! I had nothing to hold on to and I couldn't swim!

My mind started panicking. I knew I was at the deep end of the pool way over my head. I was vaguely aware of my heart beating madly and the blood madly racing through my veins, but I was trying to quell the intense feelings and trying not to panic. It wasn't working. I was going down.

Like a sinking ship I started taking in water as I desperately tried to reach for the side and call out for help... but somehow my panicked attempt to keep my head above water had moved me further away from the edge of the pool. I was terrified. My arms flailing aimlessly, I started bobbing up and down beneath the surface. I screamed in terror as I began choking on the water and it started to fill my lungs. By this stage I was in a total state of panic.

The last thing I remembered was seeing the water closing over the top of my head with distorted images of worried faces peering down through the water.

Next thing I remembered being gathered into strong arms then having my head gently lowered to the ground. Lying flat on my back with the sun in my eyes I vaguely heard a man's voice saying, "It's ok, she's going to be ok."

I looked up into the face of my rescuer and was devastated to see that it wasn't my dad. I slowly turned my head and saw both of my parents sitting next to each other a short distance away, watching me in shocked silence. I knew my Mum didn't like the water, so I never considered the thought that she didn't try to save me at all. But why didn't Dad make the effort to save me?

A belief was born in that moment that I wasn't important enough for my Dad to save me. It never occurred to me that he was probably experiencing an intense emotional response which at the time immobilized him into a state of disbelieving shock.

In my state of shock, I formulated a belief that he didn't save me because I wasn't worthy. This belief created unwanted resistance and many emotional responses in the years to follow. And the more I thought about what was wrong with me, the more reasons I "found" to reinforce that belief. Of course, most of those reasons were manufactured (and enhanced) in my own imagination.

It's amazing how fickle the mind can be... it's either working for us or working against us. And the outcome is determined moment by moment by our thoughts, the various emotions which are then triggered by those thoughts and the resulting resistance we have to experiencing those unwanted negative thoughts and feelings.

Can you see that without neutralizing mental mayhem, the ensuing effects and consequences can quickly snowball out of control?

Beliefs are just thoughts which we constantly repeat to ourselves.

Mischief and Havoc

Kristen enjoyed the close family life which I had always dreamed of having myself. Even though my mother did her best to provide emotional support and entertainment for me, she was an indoors type of person whereas I constantly craved being and playing outdoors. And I could count the number of times my Dad played with me or involved himself in my life on one hand!

One of those rare times was when he taught me how to ride a bike. I remember feeling the tension and excitement build when he mentioned off-hand that there was something for me in the garage. I raced downstairs and discovered my shiny new bike. It felt so good to have his unreserved attention, his smile beaming from ear to ear.

What made it more of a treasure was the fact that Dad didn't smile very often but that was one moment in time when I truly felt connected with him. He then took it upon himself to teach me how to be a confident rider. This precious time with Dad made me feel special and loved.

When I was younger, and he was watching TV (and I didn't feel the familiar uncomfortable resistance emanating from him) I would climb onto his chair with him for a cuddle. I would try and match my breathing with his, so I wouldn't get evicted. Then when he eventually asked me to move, sometimes I would pretend to be asleep, almost purring with contentment when he carried me down the hallway to my bedroom and tucked me into bed with my bear.

I so craved those rare moments of connection with my Dad. But he had his own problems connecting with others, so these were few and far between.

The only times I saw Dad really happy was when his son, my older brother Martyn came to visit. Our family tree was more like a family shrub with Martyn and two older brothers being from Dad's first marriage. Martyn is 13 years older than me and was thought of as "the black sheep" of the first brood. Since I was the naughty one in Dad's second marriage, Martyn and I enjoyed a close affinity and he was my idol. The fact that our birthdays were only seven days apart made him all the more special in my eyes.

We always laughed at the fact that out of his two marriages 15 years apart, Dad had five children with birthdays on the 8th, 9th and 10th of April and the 16th and 23rd of July. How cool is that?

Martyn was constantly playing pranks on my sister and me. We lived in a two-story house which Dad had built and he had strung a hammock between two upright posts underneath the deck. One day, Tania was lying in the hammock reading a book. With an eye on taking over the hammock, Martyn mischievously called out from around the corner, "Tania, your mother wants you." I had been not so patiently waiting for Tania to evacuate the hammock and leapt into it the moment she got out. A moment later, Martyn strode around the corner. "Ha!" I thought, "I beat you to it! You won't fool me that easily next time!"

A few minutes later came a call from upstairs. "Jacqui, come and help your Mum cut up some cake." Always a sucker for anything that involved food, I raced upstairs for the piece of cake which I knew would be waiting for me as payment for my help. When I breathlessly arrived in the kitchen I was so impatient to help so I could get back to my coveted position in the hammock. Mum looked at me with a bewildered expression on her face. "What cake?" she said.

Oh no! I dashed down the stairs and outside and there was Martyn with a contented Garfield expression on his face, lying in *my* hammock with his foot casually draped over the side, saying, "You fell for that one, didn't you?" He was exasperatingly good fun and it was always disappointing to see him leave.

My Dad's biggest passion was training racehorses. We had horses grazing in the paddocks at the back of our house. I often mentioned to Dad that I was interested in learning to ride horses, but he never replied so I tried to dispel that desire and instead entertained myself by riding the new bicycle he had given me. Eventually Dad added sheep into the paddocks. Dad used to make and sell fire extinguishers and when he sold the local rights of his business he had to travel out of our district to make sales. He had a passion for taking "shortcuts" along the long, country back roads and would frequently come across lambs which had been abandoned or lost by their mothers. On several occasions, he would bring home a lost, sick lamb and we would try to nurse it back to health.

The first two lambs were too weak to save, however, the next one had a determined streak which soon catapulted him into great health and vitality.

"Bertie" was like me, born with a great appetite which could never be filled. Every morning at 7:05 AM he would bleat at the top of his voice, "FEED ME!" This became my job. Even on cold winter mornings I would bundle myself up with a warm jacket and scarf, with the bottle of heated milk firmly grasped in one hand and take it down to the paddock to feed him. He would greedily chug away at the bottle with his stumpy tail wagging and loudly burp in appreciation when he had emptied the bottle.

About four weeks later Dad brought home another lamb and we named him "Bobby". In comparison to the ever-increasing girth of Bertie, Bobby was tiny. Although remaining tiny, he too quickly gained in health and vitality. We could just as easily have called him "Bounce". Whereas Bertie would waddle along with his fat contented belly, Bobby was like a happy bouncing spring on four legs!

Dad surprised us all one day when he brought home five pregnant ewes. Within a few weeks, they all gave birth and we then had seven happy lambs bouncing around the paddock. Dad and I used to lean against the tractor and watch as the lambs would race to the opposite side of the paddock then race back again. Bobby and "Tinkerbell" (who looked like twins and were inseparable friends) were always leading the way with Bertie well at the rear, contented to finish way behind the rest of the mob.

Helping Dad look after the lambs became another shared passion until one evening just as night began to fall, a couple of men drove a truck up to the gate of the paddock. Realizing what might be going on, my sister and I dashed outside and did our best to foil their attempt to round up the sheep, so they couldn't take them away. We were totally devastated. While the adult sheep had for the most part ignored us, the lambs had become our treasured friends. While Mum and Dad had both been raised on farms, as town kids, sheep farming was new to us and we hadn't emotionally balanced the idea of our naive pet lambs unwittingly being led to the slaughter...

I spent a lot of time with Kristen and her family. Her family enjoyed an active lifestyle with many weekends and hours spent boating on the water and swimming in the water. When I told Kristen my story about having nearly drowned (and the fact that I still wasn't able to swim) she and her Dad took it upon themselves to teach me how to feel confident in the water.

My own Dad's idea of teaching me how to swim was to extend his arm to support my weight just below my chest on his hand while he buoyed me up and used his other hand to push my face down under water! For someone who had nearly drowned, not the ideal procedure! This unwanted sequence caused an intense sense of panic as I desperately tried to bring my head up to where I could breathe but I couldn't because he was holding it down. I felt such resistance to his technique and fought him tooth and nail! My memory of having nearly drowned as clear as if it had happened yesterday and it was only a matter of time before Dad gave up with frustration in his only attempt to teach me how to swim.

However, with Kristen and her dad's sequential procedure, their gentle coercion and her brothers all encouraging me, I quickly gained confidence in my new-found abilities and soon enjoyed being in the water as much as they did.

It's interesting how a good procedure combined with encouragement can make all the difference in generating self-confidence and increasing self-esteem.

Many of the times I spent with Kristen and her family were the happiest moments in my childhood. At a time when town and cities within our country were still semi-rural, Kristen and I found numerous ways to entertain ourselves. One of the most favorite pastimes we discovered was to launch ourselves on to masses of wild ginger plants on a neighboring property. These acted like a springboard and would catapult us across the garden. Laughing breathlessly, this left us feeling like we could do and be and have anything in life we wanted.

Until one day when we were unceremoniously catapulted into a hidden stream and our startled shrieks brought the owner dashing out to see what was going on. She wasn't at all impressed when she saw her garden full of flattened ginger plants! A stern telling-off signaled the end of that happy activity too, so we "gingerly" departed.

It seemed that the older we became, the more responsible we were expected to be. But we didn't want to be responsible, we were kids and we just wanted to have fun!

My sister Tania and I shared a passion for the sweetened condensed milk which Mum used as a base for her famous mayonnaise recipe. Tania cunningly devised a method of punching two holes in the bottom of the can and then we would take it in turns to greedily suck out the sickly-sweet contents until we emptied the can. Then we'd feel guilty so instead of putting the empty can in the rubbish where Mum might find it, we would put it back on the shelf and hoped Mum wouldn't notice.

This cheeky antic caused Mum a great deal of consternation and frustration when picking up several cans of condensed milk from the shelf and not one of them containing any contents! We'd be standing in the kitchen surreptitiously stealing glances at each other and trying to look innocent. Unbelievably we got away with this for a while... until one day she was in less of a hurry to finish preparing dinner and thoroughly examined one of the cans.

Isn't it interesting how we are often in such a rush that we choose to ignore an obvious problem? This frequently happens in our haste to get a task completed. However, because our mind is so busy thinking of other things, we forget that problem until we encounter it again. This results in frustration, tension and resistance when the problem remains unresolved.

If you have a problem, deal with the problem and you no longer have a problem.

Rules, Boundaries and Limitations

I used to spend a lot of time in the bush which grew adjacent to the school and my house. One of the boys from my neighborhood, Will and I used to spend hours panning for gold in the stream located in the bush behind his house. This fun activity would keep us entertained for hours. His mother used to nurse injured birds back to full health and we were also given the important duty of finding worms to feed them with. These were happy, momentous times for me, times when I felt I had purpose in my life.

Will had a dog named Tangi, a lively beast who used to race alongside cars driving up to the top of the hill and then return at a jog, her tongue lolling to the side of her mouth to wait for the next car. Sometimes she would follow us in our quest for worms or for gold until she heard a car engine start nearby in which case she would dash away so she could race the car to the top of the hill. She resembled a greyhound but was taller and had semi-curly soft, long brown fur and mischievous brown eyes.

In her enthusiasm to catch up and overtake cars she would take a running leap and sail over whichever fence or gate was in her way, landing smoothly and powering away in her unwavering determination to beat that car to the top of the hill. She was hilarious, a reliable source of entertainment and laughter for all who observed her in action.

Even though my parents enforced strict boundaries for my sister and I, the vast areas of bush within our neighborhood quickly became my special places of refuge. Whenever I felt alone, judged or misunderstood, I would run into the bush and seek solace there. I'd listen to the birds, feel the cool air on my skin, dangle my bare feet in the cool waters of the creek, feel the varying textures of the bark on the trees behind my back and decide that life wasn't so bad after all.

I remember one time at school when I was blamed for something I hadn't done. Accusations flew fast and furious as I hotly debated my innocence. It wasn't my fault! When our teacher stepped in and reprimanded me, I felt that it was the final straw. It wasn't long after our lambs had been taken away from us and I was still feeling disconnected and alone. In my sensitive state, my constant thoughts about that event had already been over-whelming me as well as the related emotions I had tried not to feel.

Unabashedly crying with additional frustration, I dashed into the bush and went into hiding. Immedi-ately I was in the bush I started feeling more relaxed and connected. But then I started contemplating what had happened and I began having indignant thoughts and then thoughts of rebellion. Hearing teachers and other students calling out for me, I de-cided to ignore them and go deeper into hiding. I figured I would teach them all a lesson!

Having spent hours as a child blending into the bush pretending that I had super-powers and that I could be invisible, it was easy for me to evade detec-tion. Sometimes someone would pass within a hair-breadth of me and I would hold my breath, remain silently still and avoid being detected.

They gave up before I did. A couple of hours lat-er, I nonchalantly walked back into class and sat down at my desk. Everyone stared at me, but no-one said a word. Apparently, someone else had owned up to being responsible for what I had been accused of, yet the teacher never once apologized to me!

It's odd when you know an apology should be forthcoming, but it never arrives. What's worse though is when nothing further is said, and you therefore don't know where you stand. It's interest-ing that so many times as humans we say nothing in the hope that an issue will become resolved without further communication. But sometimes that lack of communication causes further problems.

Self-esteem is like a rock. It takes several components to transform into solid state yet constant erosion will wear it away. Truth not communicated is one of the fastest ways to erode self-esteem.

Even though we lived right next door to the school, my parents never attended sports days or family days or any other days of any importance to me. I would search the crowd for a glimpse of either or both parents, desperately hoping that one day they would come and watch me succeed. I didn't often win, but I was always in the top three.

I was desperate to be noticed, to feel valued and to be acknowledged but they were never there. It devastated me because we lived so close to the school. What valid reason could they have for not attending? The constant mental analysis of this fact added to my belief of not being worthy.

Because of this, I turned to my second family. Because I felt isolated and confused, Kristen's family had become my second family and my source of refuge. Her home had become my second home. Kristen's whole family always attended family days, her three younger brothers as well as both parents. Any opportunity to see their kids in action and to support their endeavors, her parents always made an effort to be there to cheer them on.

Looking back, I don't remember ever communicating to my parents how much I wanted them to attend school family days and sports days. If I had said something out loud (instead of just thinking it) perhaps they would have understood how important it was for me to have them there to support me.

How can you get what you want if you don't ask for it?

It hadn't been in my parents' expectations to have a child who required so much attention. My sister was highly independent and was rarely involved in sports. Tania spent most of her time happily reading or playing with her dolls inside. She experienced contentment just being by herself. She excelled intellectually and at music and art. All through school she was the model student, quiet, polite and dedicated to her studies.

Not like me at all. I was constantly chasing acknowledgment and reassurance. While Tania used to enjoy her own company, I used to worry a lot about being left alone. Maybe this need I had stemmed back to when I was a sick, allergic baby who experienced such resistance to life and constantly needed reassuring.

I seemed to have a hard time asking for what I wanted. It was like I was starving myself literally and figuratively. I was always hungry, but I didn't want to eat the raw carrots and the peanut butter sandwiches which I had asked for and my mother had packed for me. I remember one time when Kristen and I tried to coerce a couple of kids to part with their lunch. We were both tall, opinionated children and probably came across as intimidating to those who were smaller than us.

Those kids reported our behavior to a teacher and Kristen and I were made to stand up in the middle of class assembly where we were humiliated. The teacher explained in detail what we had represented to the rest of the class. She described us as being bullies. I hadn't thought of it that way and was so embarrassed and mortified that I never did anything like it ever again.

For the most part thereafter, I used to stand up for others. Because I was taller and stronger than most, I would strongly defend my perspective and that of someone else if I thought they didn't deserve to be picked on.

I would physically fight those who dared to tease me about my appearance or the slight shaking in my hands which I couldn't control. That tremor which still plagues me to this day. Growing up in a neighborhood of boys definitely had its advantages. I soon developed the reputation of being someone you didn't mess with.

Unfortunately, this tough attitude I had, prevented others from becoming close to me and kept me feeling isolated. Girls were intimidated by my strong words or actions and boys were either intimidated or in awe of me for similar reasons. This didn't translate into having many friends, rather that I just knew people. The few friends I had were like gold.

Living next door to the primary school created many opportunities to interact with other kids. Although there was a core of kids who frequented the playground, occasionally some kid from a neighboring area would present themselves. Not all of them were friendly.

I remember one time when my sister and I became involved in some sort of debate with one of those other kids. I can't even remember how it started. It was unlike Tania to make cheeky comments (that was more my thing) so I'm not quite sure how it started. However, it wasn't long before this obviously much older boy was twisting and pulling on her hair and tormenting us both with his vicious remarks. He was bigger and stronger than me so my futile attempts to rescue her failed. He just swatted me to the side like an irritating bug.

"Get Dad!" Tania desperately called out to me as she was being yanked around by her tormentor. I raced home with a dedication and speed Tangi would have been proud of, arriving breathlessly at the garage underneath the house where dad was tinkering with one of his fire extinguishers. "Tania needs help!" I exclaimed, "A tall blonde boy is dragging her and pulling on her hair!"

With that, Dad dropped the crescent he was holding and bolted out the door. Dad had been a champion sprinter when he was younger, but his speed and agility were still impressive! As I hurried to keep up, he returned to my line of sight just in time for me to see him racing toward them at full speed. As he arrived at the scene he bellowed at the blonde boy to let go of Tania. On hearing an obviously angry adult male voice the boy dropped her and started to bolt for the far gate. Changing tact, Dad took off after him and reached him within a few quick strides. Having also been a star rugby player, he mercilessly tackled him to the ground.

When the boy tried to scramble to his feet, Dad stood up and grabbed him by the hair. In an unorthodox move, he then swung the boy around a few times by his hair and then let him fly. "That will teach you not to pull on girl's hair and pick on those who are younger than you!" he stated firmly. He then turned around and trotted back to us to make sure that Tania was ok. We were totally awestruck.

The boy who had tormented Tania had been flung five feet and landed unceremoniously in a heap on the grass. He stood up, angrily flicking the grass from his shirt. "You're not going to get away with this!" he yelled and stormed off the field back in the direction he had come from. We ignored him and walked home together. That in itself, was a triumphant occasion.

About two hours later there was a loud knock at the door. I nervously reported to Dad that the blonde boy and a man who appeared to be his father were at the door. The man pounded on the door again demanding in a loud voice to speak to Dad. We all went downstairs, Dad and Tania and I. Dad opened the garage door, inviting the father to further the discussion about his son's behavior.

"My son's behavior?" he asked incredulously. "My son reports that you picked him up by the hair and threw him several feet!"

"Yes, I did," my father answered calmly. "Did he tell you that it was *after* he dragged my daughter around the playground by her hair?"

The boy's father swiveled his head toward his son saying, "You didn't tell me *that* part!" He then clipped his son around the ears and apologized profusely for his son's behavior. We never saw that boy again.

I would sometimes wonder what caused that boy to be so mean. What was going on in his life to make him react so violently?

It wasn't until many years later that I would come to the realization that it's our unresolved emotional responses which keep us cycling through unresolved behaviors. That which you resist will always persist. Some become stuck in cycles of anger, others anxiety, others frustration and others in fear.

I was always an active kid, roller skating, biking, skateboarding, playing various ball games, leaping off tall buildings. You name it, I did it... and often suffered the consequences!

Back when I was in Kindergarten, my mother had enrolled me in a gymnastics class. I remember bouncing on one of the trampolines while watching an older girl on the trampoline next to mine. She was doing backwards, and forward somersaults and I was so impressed with how much fun that appeared to be, I thought I would try one myself.

Unfortunately, I hadn't been shown the procedure for this. I bounced, landed on the springs, BO-ING! then somersaulted face first onto the floor. Smashed all my baby teeth and that was the end of gymnastics classes!

As I became older, all my adult teeth come through unevenly which didn't help with my confidence concerning my appearance.

Fast forward to age 10, all the combined events to date hadn't caused me to lose my sense of adventure.

My new classmate Rebecca and I used to roller skate down an enormous and steep hill near her house. We skated down the middle of the road (because we figured it was safer than roller skating over the bumps on people's driveways) and we frequently passed cars coasting down the hill - as they had brakes and we didn't! We both got a huge kick out of glancing into the car at the driver as we careered past them at great speed, laughing at their startled expressions as we raced to the bottom of the hill.

Just like Tangi, we would do it again and again and again and again, and never tire of the thrill. It was awesomely good fun.

Never had a mishap on that hill. This is why you wouldn't believe what happened next. One sunny day, I had just put my skates on... and launched myself into my first step... and was stopped in my tracks by a tiny small stone. Face first, I kissed the concrete. Oh no, not again! I knocked my front teeth so hard that one adult tooth went dead (black) and I had to have the nerve removed. That was an excruciating process as part of the nerve wasn't at all dead and the dentist hadn't used enough anesthetic.

Back in those days, cosmetic dentistry was a failure. I ended up with braces on my teeth for eight years. They had removed the dead tooth and tried to shuffle my other teeth around, so I had a somewhat even smile. But they removed too many teeth and when the braces finally came off, a gap appeared between my front tooth and the little tooth they had moved into the other front tooth position.

I was sooooo self-conscious of my smile. I would rearrange my tongue behind my teeth when I smiled, trying to disguise the gap between my teeth. Along with growing up being tall, flat-chested and slim, I had frizzy hair, a big nose, and braces. There wasn't much about my appearance which made me feel good about myself.

There are certain elements which breed confidence, self-esteem and a sense of belonging. Few of them have anything to do with appearance. But I didn't know that then. And so, I continued to believe my lack of acceptance to be something which was beyond my control.

On the Outside, Looking In

When we reached middle school (intermediate school) Rebecca was zoned for a different school and Kristen and I were separated into different classes. After the familiarity of primary school where everyone knew each other, I felt like I was a Star Trek captain in an alien environment. Unlike Kristen, I wasn't so good at making friends and it took a long time to stop resisting the fact that we weren't in the same class.

Somehow, I needed to move forwards and create a new life for myself, but I didn't know how.

It always seemed that everyone else had friends, that everyone else belonged. Even when I was accepted into a group I felt like I was on the outside looking in. I felt like I was just being tolerated, like I didn't really belong. Why did I always feel so separate? I thought my upcoming overseas trip might give me some more "status" and credibility.

That year, I went on a six-week holiday to the USA and Canada with my Mum and sister. Dad hadn't wanted to go so it was just the three of us. My friends Kristen and Rebecca had been invited for a sleep over a couple of days before we left for our trip. It was my 12th birthday and they each gave me a huge slab of chocolate for my birthday! Along with the king-size bar of chocolate my Dad had given me, I now had three. Not thinking anything of ramifications, I threw the chocolate bars on top of the clothes packed into my suitcase and contemplated the attitude my sister would have toward me as she tried to "lighten" me of some of my chocolate!

We were both in for a rude awakening when we made it to Los Angeles. 18 hours later, after a stop-off at Honolulu we excitedly opened my suitcase to discover that the three large packets of chocolate had melted their way through my entire suitcase full of clothes. Probably the first example of edible undies? What a rude start to our holiday! Mum was not impressed. She went in search of the hotel laundry while we went in search of the pool.

I was at that awkward age where I was still a kid but wanted to feel and act like a grown-up. Because of this I missed out on a lot of fun I could have otherwise experienced as I kept myself separate from other children. I just hadn't figured out how to relax, enjoy myself and feel confident interacting with others.

During our whole time spent in the USA and Canada, I was absolutely fascinated by squirrels. I would spend hours trying to entice wild squirrels to come up to me. Once, one of them came up and thought my finger was the treat as it hadn't occurred to me to hold out something for the little critter to eat.

Watching and interacting with the innocence of Nature's creatures provides such a wonderful reprieve from our constant thoughts.

I wished that I had the ability to get on with humans as well as I did with animals. I had always felt such a strong affinity with animals and their joyful, carefree antics. Without fear of judgment or reprieve, I wouldn't hesitate to approach an animal and would often make it my mission to befriend it if it appeared to be somewhat shy. It's odd that I never thought of taking that same approach with humans until much later in life. I guess I figured everyone else had it more together than I did, and it didn't occur to me that there were many others who were feeling as lonely as I was.

It's interesting how we keep ourselves isolated with our erroneously, preconceived and imagined observations.

Due to viewing myself as being socially inept, the rest of my school years were challenging for me. I did make other friends however, at the end of intermediate school my closest friends (including Kristen) all moved to distant locations.

Suddenly it was time to start high school. Suddenly I wasn't one of the students at the top of the class, now I was just one of many. It felt like I was being consumed entirely by the enormity of my sense of separation. A whole new bunch of people to tease me about my frizzy hair and braces. More teasing about my shaking hands. Some of the cruel jokes and remarks made by the older students were almost laughable but I still took them on board personally because I felt insecure about myself.

Even though I argued and fought to preserve my pride, many of these other kids were bigger than me and fought in packs like wolves. I felt like I had lost that slim advantage I previously held.

Without that strong sense of kinship and camaraderie I had with Kristen and Rebecca, I felt myself slipping. I started losing my sense of direction. After spending most of my childhood chasing attention and approval from my father by achieving good grades and through sporting accomplishments, I eventually gave up and changed tack.

Seeking attention and not getting it anywhere I started playing up and being disruptive in class. Initially it was just one class. Social studies. I vehemently hated my social studies teacher, she was an argumentative, self-righteous piece of work who seemed determined to make my life in her class a misery. And the topic itself was supposed to engender compassion!

Teachers need to be trained to recognize that teens who develop behavior problems usually have a reason for it. This would go a long way to preventing teen suicides. Adults tend to assume that misbehavior is related to teen hormones and being "at that age" whereas in most cases there are many levels and layers of emotional resistance which aren't being identified or coped with. Combined with teens not having the advanced mental, verbal or emotional skills to deal with issues of personal importance, this becomes an ongoing recipe for disaster.

Because there is little general education provided to the masses to advance our knowledge of social and communication skills, we tend to inherit our people relationship skills from our life's experiences. This is why, along with suppressing our emotional responses, if life hasn't taught us how to relate effectively, we become walled off from others and shut off from our natural ability to feel good about living.

This is what happened to me and because of it I started thinking that most of school was crap, that the lessons weren't relevant to the real life which I wanted to participate in. I was feeling a growing sense of separatism between myself, my teachers, and my classmates. I started regularly skipping school.

I hadn't completely lost my desire to learn, I had simply lost my desire to actively participate in school. Most of the subjects bored me and the teachers' unenthusiastic delivery of their subject matter bored me. They just couldn't ignite my interest. Perhaps this was exacerbated by my growing sense of separation. I also hated the school uniform as well as the constant rules and regulations which smothered my natural desire to feel unencumbered and free.

The only thing which made school tolerable was my involvement in various sporting activities which included badminton, soccer and volleyball. I continued to be fiercely competitive. Although I had loved to play softball at primary school, a group of the kids who bullied me at intermediate and high school were the ones who were involved in softball. Due to my developing a super-sensitivity to their words directed at me, I figured it was easier to just avoid that activity even though I had dreamed of playing the game at a national level!

It's sad that we allow a fear of failure, a fear of not doing something right, or a fear of not performing up to someone else's standard to prevent us from doing what would naturally make our heart sing. As it is only in doing things for ourselves which enable us to feel fulfilled as human beings.

One activity that did restore some confidence in myself was a life-saving course taking place at the school swimming pool. One of my classmates suggested I might want to sign up for it with her. While I had grown to enjoy spending time in the water and had total confidence swimming a length of the pool completely under water, I wasn't what I would consider to be a strong swimmer. Especially at surf beaches which had massive waves and dangerous rips and undercurrents.

My absolute favorite beach was Muriwai where my dad trained his racehorse. My parents had purchased a small cottage out at the beach and Dad would spend many weekends out there in summer and autumn, building the horse's strength and stamina in time for the winter steeple chasing events.

Before Kristen moved away, almost every weekend in summer we would drive out to the beach. Dad would check on the horses then Tania and Kristen and I would race into the waves for a swim while Mum laid out a picnic lunch on the beach.

The lifeguards would advise everyone to stay swimming between the flags. Unless you were a strong swimmer it wasn't advisable to go out deeper than about mid-thigh level as one large wave would immediately increase the depth to your chin. With the strong undertow beneath, it would then make it challenging to retain a strong grip in the sand with your toes. The rip was so dangerous at this beach that one day after we had left, two people drowned and the next day someone else drowned also.

Still feeling lucky from our narrow escape, a year or so before (which could so easily have been us), when my new classmate suggested the life-saving course I immediately signed up!

The course became a savior for me by restoring some confidence and self-belief. I still wasn't all that comfortable submerging my face in the water to do the arm over arm crawl probably because I never really figured out how to coordinate my breathing. However, I mastered side-stroke and for enhanced life-saving capabilities that was the most important stroke of all.

Within two years, I passed the junior, then the intermediate, then the senior life-saving courses, passed my CPR and mouth-to-mouth life-saving certificate and had absolute confidence in my ability to tow another person in a one-mile swim and revive them at the end of it.

Little did I know that this skill would be called upon in future.

It was about this time that I met Rachel. She lived not far from me near the opposite boundary of the school grounds where I lived. Although not interacting friends in high school, after school and in the weekends, we would hang out.

Sometimes Rachel and I would sit and talk as we watched a group of boys who lived in a nearby neighborhood. They came to the neighboring school after school hours to play ball games including touch rugby and cricket. While I had watched these boys play for years, they had never invited me to play.

One particularly sunny afternoon Rachel and I were sitting on the boundary of the playing field discussing the foibles of life when out of the corner of my eye I saw the cricket ball cannoning towards me at a great rate.

"Ha!" I thought, "This is my opportunity to prove that I'm good enough!" In the moment the ball was about to sail over my head, I casually reached my right hand up and plucked it out of the air. Cheers and applause erupted from the boys on the playing field.

"Jacqui! We didn't know you could play! You should come and have a bat?"

Now I was in my element. Having been a great lover of batting in softball and actively participating in many sports, I felt totally confident in my ability as I approached the cricket pitch. Because I was a girl, they started with a slow ball. I advanced down the wicket to meet the ball and WHACK!! Smashed it out of the playing field.

"Ahhhhh..." Stephan, the bowler said. "So, you know how to play. Let's try a faster ball." WHACK! I hit it even further out of the field. Now the boys were starting to feel intimidated. They brought in their fastest bowler. I just kept hitting the ball right out of the playing field.

Ten minutes later some excuse was made, and I was banished unceremoniously to the sidelines. While I thought I had been impressing them, in reality I was alienating myself. Because I was showing them up (another GIRL was watching) and they felt embarrassed that they were being outplayed by a girl.

The only times I received an invite to play from that point on was when they needed an extra player to balance the numbers. Interestingly, because they considered me to be a friend of Rachel (and one of them liked Rachel) I became somewhat included in their non-sport activities at the school near where we all lived.

The most prominent of these activities included my introduction to alcohol. I was only 13. After all the years of not being able to find the words to communicate my needs, alcohol seemed to provide me with some much-needed personality. Or so I thought. While I thought alcohol made me more socially acceptable, in reality it continued to push potential new friends away.

But at this stage when my inability to relate and connect was mentally and emotionally pushing me over the edge, alcohol appeared to be the only thing which offered some non-judgmental relief. So, I drank lots of it. I knew I was on the path to becoming a wayward teenager by smoking, drinking and getting into trouble. However, these activities provided a much-needed distraction from my constant negative thoughts as well as providing an emotional feeling fix. I desperately wanted to feel better, but I had no pertinent skills which enabled me to do so.

While other kids my age saved their pocket money for clothes and teen magazines, I started saving mine for cigarettes and alcohol. Suddenly I wasn't quite so alone anymore, alcohol had become my new friend. A bottle of booze made me feel like I was connected to something friendly, so I held onto it for grim life.

My parents hardly touched alcohol so Rachel and I used to sneak some out of her parents' liquor cabinet and she would also help her parents "lose" the odd packet of cigarettes. I would crave the sensation of inhaling smoke into my lungs and crave the numbing effect alcohol would have on my brain. Anything to stop the anxiety that I would never be able to feel fulfilled as a human being!

The problem was that I overindulged. I didn't just stop at one or two drinks, I would drink myself into oblivion given any opportunity. Even though I desperately tried to portray myself as someone who was cool, contained and in control, my drinking painted an entirely different picture. I was most definitely spiraling into a destructive nosedive.

I didn't drink for fun or to enhance how I was feeling, I drank to escape from the thoughts of separation and unworthiness which were constantly tormenting me. There was nothing I wanted more than to feel like I fitted in. Yet the more I tried to connect to others from that place of isolation, the more obvious it became that my strategy to connect wasn't working at all! And because I didn't have the skills to communicate my need to be heard, to feel appreciated and to feel like I belonged, I continued to feel overwhelmed with despair and continued reaching for my fake, make-believe, substitute friend, alcohol.

At the end of that school year Rachel moved away too. Before she left, she introduced me to a new girl in our extended (surrounding the school) neighborhood, Melanie. Recently having moved from a rural town, she was a year younger than me and as open to as much experimentation with alcohol as I was.

Being a teenager is a confusing time. You want to grab hold of all life has to offer but often your choices are constricted when you perceive yourself as being unworthy. Instead of seeing what the world has to offer, you struggle to survive moment by moment because of the constant tug-of-war going on in your own mind.

There were so many things that I wanted to do and try but I thought I needed friends to engage in the activities.

It was many years before I would come to the conclusion that life was to be lived by me for me, that if I wanted something then it was up to me to fulfil that dream.

When I was 14, Melanie and I plus another friend or two used to go to a local underage nightclub. Because I was tall and looked older than I was, I would walk across to the bottle store on the other side of the road and buy a couple of bottles of wine. We'd then stand in the car park of the underage nightclub and knock back those bottles within 5 minutes, pop a mint in our mouths to freshen our breath and slyly stride into the nightclub.

From a young age, I had and still have a fascination with dancing. Back then it was one of the few times I always felt truly alive, vibrant and free. However, impaired by the alcohol now contaminating my brain, my natural rhythm was lost and what had once been a source of confidence and joy became a sense of disorientation and embarrassment. The fact that all the boys hit on Melanie and seemed totally unaware of my presence added to my growing sense of unease and isolation.

All my friends seemed to be able to attract boys, what was wrong with me? I just couldn't figure it out. While my friends found it so easy to chat and interact, I didn't know what to say. Often, I would just stand there, looking and feeling mute and invisible. I didn't know it at the time but in that respect, I was simply lacking in social interactive skills. Hopefully one day these will be an essential subject taught as part of every school's curriculum.

I remember one time when a group of us made a trip to the hot pools. It was one of those times when

I had been mentally beating up on myself, feeling like I didn't fit in and generally allowing my thoughts to make myself feel miserable. Melanie and the others had befriended a group of boys and they were all laughing and splashing and having a great time. Instead of taking a moment to experience that brief awareness of feeling shy and awkward and then joining in, I once again kept myself separate.

Their new friends probably wondered why I was being aloof! I didn't mean to be, I just couldn't bring myself to bridge that intense bout of resistance I was experiencing. It was like there was an invisible barrier preventing me from crossing over into happiness and fun. Even as I watched them having fun, I continued to sink myself into a pit of negativity. I made myself separate, I made myself alone. I observed myself doing this. The more time I had alone with my thoughts, the worse state I sunk myself into. It was as though I had an addiction to feeling sorry for myself at this point of my life and to being, a victim.

Remember that your conscious mind lies, cheats and makes excuses whenever you allow it to.

I'll never forget one time when I was about 15. I was sitting in Art class, Mr Dobson was my teacher. He was one of those rare people who would really pay attention and listen to what you were saying. He didn't talk down to you but made you feel valued and understood as a person and was popular among the students.

In class that day we had to partner up with someone else and then draw a portrait of each other. I remember at that time of my life my self-esteem was at an all-time low. I felt super self-conscious and depressed about the way I looked - and made some throwaway comment about it.

Mr Dobson was sitting nearby. He looked me in the eye and said, "You know what, Jacqui? You have great facial bone structure. By the time, you get to your late thirties you'll start coming into your own and your looks will continue to improve with age. While many of your classmates may look good now, they will be *losing* their looks at that age. Whereas yours will keep improving."

That kindness carried me through some very dark times in my life before I learned how to allow an emotional response to pass. (Doing that one thing was what changed my life forever.)

There were only a few classes which I enjoyed in high-school. Art and photography were two of them. Mr Dobson taught both. Unlike most of my teachers who were highly strung, reactive and volatile, Mr Dobson had an easy going, relaxed kind of nature which always provided a relaxed and fun learning experience. It was interesting that no one ever played up in his classes.

I remember one time the following year when I sneaked out of photography class to have a smoke in the washroom. I didn't really want one, but it had become my habit to deal with any brief emotional response by having a cigarette. Unfortunately, my timing was off, I was sprung by another teacher and unceremoniously marched back to my class. When she saw Mr Dobson (who was known for being soft on student punishment) she haughtily informed him that I should be suitably punished for my misdemeanor. When she left, I admitted that it was my third time being caught smoking which meant automatic suspension and, so I might as well go home now.

He just said, "Well, I can tell she's going to follow up on this, so I have to prove that you've been suitably punished. Let's see how we can get around this so you don't have to miss out on school." He paused in a moment of deep reflective thought, then grabbed a detention slip from a drawer in his desk and scrawled out an indecipherable description then signed his name to it. "There you go," he said, "They'll have a hard time trying to figure that one out!"

That was the most awesome thing about Mr Dobson, he never criticized any of us and he seemed to have a genuine understanding of how rough it can be to survive school and life. As a wayward and disconnected teen, I never felt judged by him, always felt supported and appreciated having an adult who always appeared to support me. He made my latter years at high school almost enjoyable.

My parents had an interesting way of dealing out punishment when it was warranted. While Dad didn't have much time for us, he also rarely displayed anger against our actions. The second time I had been caught smoking I had been marched to the Dean's office where he promptly called my parents. I knew Mum was at work and smugly thought I had evaded trouble so was mortified when Dad answered the phone. It was one of the rare occasions when Dad was actually home. Now I would be in serious trouble! The Dean put the phone on speaker and I was absolutely stunned when after explaining my bad deed, Dad simply laughed and said, "I've already been through this with three sons, it's not a big deal. She'll decide one day that it's no good for her and she'll make the decision to stop."

I was still somewhat nervous when I arrived home, knowing I still had Mum to deal with. She just said to me, "So you were caught smoking. I thought I had smelt that on you. I'm disappointed, but it's your choice. If you want to ruin your life, then that's up to you." This acknowledgment of her disappointment in me had much more of an impact than a beating ever could.

In the past, Mum had been the one to dish out serious punishments with one whack of a wooden spoon. When Tania and I were caught out for a mutual misdemeanor Tania would get it first because she was older and should have known better. The large wooden spoons were weak from stirring many great pots of jams and preserves so they usually broke on Tania and I was let off with a stern warning. Then, depending on the extent of our mischief we would be sent to our rooms as further punishment.

One time, Dad tried using the soft leather part of one of his belts on Tania and was mortified when it left a big red welt. That was the first and last time the belt was used. The next time Mum decided we needed further punishment beyond scolding we were taken down to the bottom of the stairwell where Dad's punishments were carried out. Dad ordered Tania to hold her hands out in front of her with her palms facing up. Dad would then bring his hands down and slap her on her hands, really hard. I had experienced it once and it was surprising how much it hurt.

However, this new method of punishment fell flat the second time we were in trouble as right at the last moment Tania quickly withdrew her hands and Dad slapped his own thighs really hard! I was standing halfway up the stairwell awaiting my turn and saw the whole event unfold before my eyes. I couldn't help myself and laughed out loud at Dad's stunned, disbelieving expression and at Tania's eyes which were lit up with mischievous delight before she realized that she was now in more serious trouble!

Because of my edgy, brazen type of personality, I never really felt as a girl. Having grown up mostly in a neighborhood full of boys (the girls were several years older than me) I continued to be competitive like the boys. I thought that if I was faster, stronger and more intelligent I would finally be accepted. It didn't work out that way.

Having felt like I was somewhere in the in-between zone, I was accepted as a friend by boys because of those male focused traits but I never fitted in with the girly girls. This was fine when I was a kid but as I grew up I watched all the boys going silly over the girly girls, but they never looked twice at me. I couldn't figure out what I was doing wrong. After all, wasn't I faster, stronger and more intelligent?

It was many years before I realized my strong "male" traits were off-putting to many males because I was too much like them. They didn't want to be in a relationship with another male, they wanted a female. And I wasn't acting like one.

While I'm still not a feminine female, I've learned how to balance these strong traits with some new skills. One thing that eventually totally transformed the image I had formed of myself was Carol Tuttle's book and online course, Dressing Your Truth. It's based on dressing to your personality type, in the styles and colors which enhance (instead of contradicting) your personality.

It's amazing how quickly insightful and simple knowledge can contribute towards transforming your opinion of yourself.

Back in the days when I was trying to be more of a girly girl and then as I became older and tried to morph into a feminine type woman, (kind of like a swordfish trying to be a mermaid) I grew my hair long and would wear long flowing skirts with soft lines and soft colors. That so wasn't me! I even felt like an imposter when wearing those clothes. Then I would open my mouth and be active, reactive, bossy and blunt. My naturally occurring movements would be swift, dynamic, motivational, let's DO IT.

I'm an action taker. Whereas those soft flowing skirts and colors engendered a softer, more gentle personality. Because of this, even as a young adult, my attempt to fit in "took a nosedive". People would smile at my obvious gentleness, then I'd open my mouth and my "get it done now" self would leap out! I would observe their expression of disbelief (or distaste) and further judge myself as being unworthy. This was until I learned how to dress my truth and to upgrade my skill set to understand how attraction works.

Emotional responses were constantly triggered when I used to think about my appearance. I'd look in the mirror and feel frustration, fear and anxiety and wonder how anyone would ever choose me when others were so much more attractive. Sometimes those emotional responses are triggered now when I analyze the additional wrinkles I've earned from my life experiences. However, now I know *exactly* what to do when I'm feeling that way.

Of course, back in those days I would try and block the physical discomfort of the emotional response because I already felt bad and didn't want to make myself feel worse. I didn't know that it was this very action which continued to keep me feeling isolated.

Phobias, Fears and Freedom

As I became older I would experience brief moments of peace and happiness from time to time, but they were always fleeting... and then I would feel alone again, once more disconnecting myself from participating in life. It seemed that nothing (and no-one) could make me feel like I belonged anywhere. It's interesting that I never really expected to neither did I make much of an effort to step out of my comfort zone and try and make new friends.

Like so many others, I always felt like I was on the outside of life looking in. At the time, I wondered why others seemed to have it so together and why they seemed happy and content as I could never arrive at that point myself.

At the age of 16, I developed a fear of driving. This wasn't helped by the fact that I had been involved in a couple of minor car accidents. I remember one day, I decided I would try to help my parents by washing the family car. I approached Mum and asked her to move the car, so I could wash it. She replied, "I'm busy, go ask your father."

So, I went and asked Dad. "Dad, can you please move the car, so I can wash it?" Would you believe it, he said just about the same thing, "I'm busy now? Go ask your mother."

Feeling nonplussed, I figured it couldn't be too hard to move the car 20 feet. I grabbed the keys, marched to the car and inserted the key in the ignition. Recalling the driving lessons, I had undertaken, I put the car into reverse, checked my mirrors and applied a bit of acceleration.

I was congratulating myself on how easy this was until I realized how close I was to my Dad's truck parked on the opposite side of the driveway. Panic! Trying to ignore my heart racing and blood pounding into my head, I wrenched the wheel to the right and accelerated - right into Dad's prized rose bushes!

I decided not to brake, wanting to get out of the danger zone (and get the car out of the vicinity of the rose bushes) as fast as possible! I wrenched the wheel to the left, missed the truck and reversed into the solid wooden sentry post at the gate. CRUNCH! In a total panic and contemplating how much trouble I was going to be in, I figured I had to at least continue and wash the car (unusual reasoning but I most certainly wasn't thinking clearly at that stage!)

I then gingerly maneuvered the car forward and to the right. Moving the manual stick into reverse, I looked over my shoulder and accidentally stomped on the accelerator instead of the brake and smashed into the sentry post on the opposite side of the gate. CRUNCH! How could such a well-meaning gesture turn out so horribly? At the additional noise, both my parents came running out of the house.

With my hands shaking uncontrollably, I tried to look innocent and focused on the fact that I had been trying to be helpful. Besides being stuck with the massive bill to repair the car, I was forgiven because of my good intention - and the fact that I *had* asked both parents to help me move the car.

The after-effect of this incident however stopped me from driving for nearly twelve years. Twelve years! First, I had to wait 3 weeks for the car to be repaired. Then I thought I would wait until after school exams. Then I thought of some other reason why I couldn't drive yet... and then another excuse... and then another.

I knew I was making excuses but every time I thought about driving a car, my mind was inundated with memories of my heart beating madly, losing my control and crashing into the gate... This left me trembling uncontrollably with a huge ball of fear and anxiety in the pit of my stomach. This is a typical example of how unresolved emotional responses resurface.

With each of those memories my heart would pound in my chest, my hands would shake... I'd try to ignore the physical discomfort and my mind would go into overdrive, questioning... judging... condemning. I wanted the freedom and independence which go hand in hand with driving, but my insecurities coaxed me out of driving for a very long time.

Surprisingly, my driving record prior to that stage had been nearly perfect. When I started my driving lessons I had thought it was fairly straightforward and easy (even though I was responsible for my Mum's first grey hairs when I frequently hit the accelerator instead of the brake during our lessons.)

But after that incident of crashing the family car I lost my confidence and allowed myself to become terrified at any thought of driving. Even though it severely handicapped my social life, I refused to drive a car for nearly twelve years.

The point of this story is to show that the incorrect emotional response for the wrong reason can contaminate a person's mind for a long time. And it wasn't until I dealt with the issue 12 years later that the problem disappeared.

Sixteen was not a sweet year for me. On the actual day that I turned 16 I was befriended by an adult neighbor, a family friend who appeared to understand me and value me as being a dynamic individual. For the first few months I experienced this new-found friendship as being absolute bliss. He would pick me up on the long walk home from school and we would laugh and joke all the way home.

But his intentions were not honorable, and it would be some time before I would realize this.

After a few months of appearing to be a staunch friend, ally and confidante during my turbulent teenage years, he turned his friendly attention on me with unsolicited sexual attention. I was mortified and didn't know how to deal with it. I couldn't cope mentally or emotionally and didn't know how to forcefully communicate my need and desire for him to stop.

Feeling helpless and unable to tell anyone due to the popularity of this man in our neighborhood, I alternated between feeling ashamed, depressed and completely overwhelmed. Like so many others who have been sexually abused, I became further withdrawn from my family and friends, my self-esteem plummeted, and my school work suffered.

This "friend" continued to abuse me sexually for over a year.

It's interesting that many sexual predators seek out children who obviously don't have friends. Instead of looking for confident prey, they pounce on those who look lonely, those whose faces are set in sadness or which contain a hard expression as they try to cope with their mental and emotional burdens. Like mine. These confused expressions communicate "I've got issues!"

These children and teens often appear to be unhappy, vulnerable and struggling. They appear to be unprotected by family or friends, they may be perceived to be "a problem child" or a trouble maker. Sexual predators tap into negative behaviors and often accentuate that opinion by commenting to others about how the child is misbehaving.

Misinterpreting my random emotional outbursts as being socially unacceptable I was misunderstood by my friends who eventually withdrew from my friendship. This was so frustrating! I became angry and insolent toward my teachers and classmates and made it difficult for others to tolerate me even though there was nothing I wanted more than to integrate and feel normal.

It constantly felt like I was on an emotional rollercoaster which never seemed to stop. Although no one knew my dreadful secret, I felt alone, judged and condemned.

When I eventually did tell my closest friends, my worst nightmare came true – they didn't believe me. They said "Mr B" was a wonderful man and that I was just saying these nasty things about him to get attention. Needless to say, I was totally devastated. I felt like giving up. Why wasn't anyone hearing my silent scream for help? It had taken many months to build up the confidence to finally confess to what was going on and I was totally crushed to be accused and blamed for wrongdoing.

To make matters worse we all worked part time in this man's business. The very thing which funded my out of school activities kept me cycling through the terror of being left alone with him, what he might do and how I would feel about it after. But I was desperate to fit in socially and having pocket money was an essential part of that plan, so I continued to work there.

Several months later my friends decided that because I was repeatedly telling them about my same plight, I couldn't be lying, and they apologized for not believing me. They promised to ensure that they would never let me be left alone with him again, without one of them being present. Although not totally solving the problem it relieved the burden of pressure I felt in keeping the secret to myself. I also felt safer within their protective shell.

During this time (and for most of my teenage years) I was constantly searching for alternate influences in a hopeful attempt to make myself feel better. I felt like I needed a confidence boost, so I smoked cigarettes and drank copious amounts of alcohol. I always looked older than I was, so it was easy for me to purchase booze.

Whereas my peers appeared to be excited to learn, to socialize and to evolve themselves as individuals, I viewed school as being tedious, boring and restrictive. This was probably due to my own self-neglect. I had not realized at that time that it was myself who was shutting myself off from feeling and enjoying and experiencing my life to the fullest.

Moments of self-acknowledgement were few and far between until I made a concerted effort to upgrade my thoughts and deal with my emotions.

My self-recriminations and judgements were stifling my natural creativity and sense of adventure. Sometimes I would totally withdraw from the company of others and sink myself into such a pit of negativity that I felt like I would surely drown. It was almost like I was trying to make myself invisible and to some extent it worked.

Because I didn't know how to communicate in such a way that I would feel heard and understood it seemed easier to keep myself aloof from others. But in doing this I alienated myself and therefore never felt like I belonged.

Kristen and her family had moved back into the neighborhood. I was called unceremoniously back into the Dean's office after Kristen's mother remarked that Kristen was a straight "A" student like Jacqui Olliver! Because that had rarely been my high school's evaluation of me, I was called in to explain the anomaly. What was keeping me from performing to the best of my ability? I asked if he wanted me to make a list...

As a child, I had always been daring but as I advanced through my teenage years my actions became dangerous and reckless. In short, I was quickly spiraling out of control. I didn't really re-connect with Kristen when she moved back as we had become two completely different people. Alcohol had become my go to "to feel good" and I would often skip school and go on a drinking binge with another socially inept outcast. Although we survived those reckless drinking and driving binges unscathed, we never gained any peace or social acceptance from our activities.

Upon returning from a lunchtime drinking excursion, other students would look at me with disbelieving then dismissive expressions which only led me to feel even more insecure and rejected. Even though I was trying to be cool, it seemed they all thought I was being melodramatic.

It's interesting the difference between how we see ourselves in the world and how others actually view us. I spent a lot of time and energy trying to pretend I was cool when in reality I was conversely portraying myself as insecure.

I continued to endure high school until I finished my time there and eventually walked away from that part of my life without further incident.

There were four of us older teens who still lived around the perimeter of the primary school. Melanie and I, and two boys the same age as Melanie. She was going out with one and I eventually started going out with the other who was his best friend. We had been friends for many years and we sort of just fell into being together.

He was amazing in so many ways however, there was one major problem for me. While I liked a kiss to be a slow exploratory entwining of tongues, it felt like he was devouring my face every time we kissed. After spending a few months together, even though I thought he was wonderful, I backed off from being in a relationship with him simply because of the way he kissed me. He was one of the most amazing guys I had ever known, and he remained a steadfast friend for many years.

A few years later I had the opportunity to get back together with him and I really wanted to but as soon as he kissed me I was reminded of that incompatibility and repelled his advances. Knowing what I know now, I simply would have communicated how I liked to be kissed so he could fulfil that need for me! It's ironic how carelessly we can throw something wonderful away when we don't know how to communicate our wants, needs and desires.

It was in furthering my life's experience which lead me to the insightful answers I share with others now. The reality is that if my life hadn't unfolded as it eventually did then I would not be who I am now and inspiring thousands of people worldwide to feel a whole lot better about living.

The unique methods I eventually developed are now endorsed by leading medical specialists (see part 2.) With my relevant sex education *answers,* I am considered by many to be a world leader in restoring emotional balance as well as full sexual function. Sex Ed isn't just about sex, it's about emotional balance, attraction alignment, sexual function and knowing how to get your needs met.

Let me explain how I arrived at that point.

As the years passed I continued to struggle to feel fulfilled as a human being. The same problem extended well into my adult years. This part of my journey was perhaps my greatest challenge. To be able to feel fulfilled as a fully functioning (emotionally and sexually) adult! How can we feel fulfilled when these essential life skills aren't taught to us by our education systems?

During my last year at high school I had started hanging out with Helen, a girl in my photography class. We had vaguely known each other all the way through school but only really became friends in our final year due to our shared love of photography. She was a die-hard punk rocker with a love of music.

Spending a lot of that summer at Helen's house it wasn't long before the drummer in her brother's band caught my eye. Jason had a mischievous, magnetic type of personality and completely charmed me. I was thrilled when he indicated that he liked me back! We started going out together.

Jason and I dated for about six months. He was a skilled and considerate lover, but he was unable to help me achieve orgasm. I didn't know it at the time, but it was I who was holding myself back. Concerning sex, I didn't have the right procedure imprinted in my brain. It would start feeling good and I would start thinking, "Is it? Is it? Is it?" and those delicious feelings would evaporate! I despaired that I would never be able to relax enough to achieve orgasm.

While Jason led a totally fulfilling life, my life felt empty when he wasn't in it. He was studying two degrees at University, was a black belt in Karate and taught drumming at the local community center. As well, he played in a band. He didn't have a lot of spare time and due to his time constraints, we eventually drifted apart. At the time, I didn't know how important it is (especially when you're in a relationship) to take the responsibility of fulfilling yourself as a person.

After excelling at secretarial studies at school I had decided to advance those studies at a local polytechnic. I had no preconceived idea of what direction I would take in life, so I chose to start with a subject I was good at. However, it wasn't long before I discovered that it didn't hold my interest. My mother had to work hard at convincing me to commit to completing the year-long course!

The most challenging aspect of the course was preparing a mandatory speech to complete a portion of the final exam. Whereas I had made excuses all the way through high school (and flatly refused to give a speech) at Polytech I had no choice because the speech was worth 30% of the year's final grade. I had never felt confident in my ability to communicate in front of others and was somewhat reluctant to put myself into that position. However, with the speech being an integral part of the year's final grade there was just no escaping it!

None of us were enthusiastic about having to deliver a speech. Still dragging our heels with obvious reluctance, we were taught the process of writing an effective speech. The subject I chose was my passion at the time, black and white photography. I wrote my speech and then spent hours in my bedroom rehearsing and repetitively vocalizing it until I felt confident I could successfully deliver it with ease.

The fateful speech delivery day arrived. With my naturally shaking hands exacerbated by the intense circumstances, I was curious to note that I felt more excited than nervous. I felt *prepared*. I gave my speech passionately and flawlessly. I received a standing ovation! Me! A standing ovation for my speech. I could hardly believe it. The examiner complimented me as it was the best speech and delivery she had heard that year. I was absolutely thrilled when six weeks later I received a certificate in the post. This informed me I had passed the Senior Level of the New Zealand Speech Board with Honors!

This proves that with the right knowledge and preparation, confidence and success can easily follow.

I decided after that year of doing Secretarial Studies it would drive me absolutely crazy if I had to work in an office! I just wasn't cut out for it. Since I was showing an obvious talent for all things related to photography I got myself a full-time job in a photo lab selling cameras as well as developing and printing photos.

After paying my parents back all the money they had loaned me over the years I was finally able to move into a house in a flatting situation with two other young adults. Oh, the freedom! With a nightclub for dancing just up the road and plenty of money to spend on booze, I thought I was in my element.

I was the first amongst my friends to move out of home. Not long after, Melanie and the two boys moved into a house together and it soon became a dedicated party venue. Every other weekend I would walk across town to their place. Like Dad, I knew every shortcut to shorten the journey and arrive in record time.

It was usual for us to spend most of the night playing cards and indulging in various drinking games. On this particular night, I was the last one standing. Bored by the fact that everyone else had "faded away," I decided to walk home. Weaving and winding my way up the road I was a little over half-way home when a guy in a car called out something I thought to be demeaning.

Taking offence, I retorted with some rude and insulting comment to which he swerved over to the sidewalk and leapt out of his car. I wasn't hanging around to hear what he had to say. He appeared to be really angry, so I just ran! Sprinting across to the opposite side of the road I made for the nearest building which happened to be a funeral parlor. "How ironic," I thought, as I dashed around the corner looking for a suitable place to hide. I could hear his footsteps quickly approaching in hot pursuit.

Thankful for all those years spent hiding in nature, I spotted a bushy tree in a garden near the side of the building. I quickly tiptoed around the edge of the flower bed careful not to give my hiding place away, then I crouched behind the tree. I purposely slowed my breathing down in an attempt to make myself less audible.

The man slowed down as he turned the corner, saying, "You can't hide from me Girlie and when I find you I'm going to enjoy hurting you." Between the long walk home and the terror of my predicament I had sobered up amazingly quickly. He came to within a hair's breadth of my hiding place. Not daring to move I called upon my childhood skill of pretending that I was as inert as a statue. I didn't flinch or twitch a muscle. Even though my heart was hammering, in the presence of such danger I felt a sense of calm wash over me.

Swearing in disgust that he couldn't find me and exact his revenge, after five long minutes which felt like a lifetime, he gave up looking for me. I could hear his footsteps moving away. Then I heard a car door slam and the sound of an engine starting up before the sound of a car driving away. I wasn't sure it was him who had left so it was another five minutes before I gingerly moved away from the safety of my hiding position. Then I raced home fearing that he would come back for me or discover me walking home.

Luckily, I made it home unscathed. Feeling like a cat minus one of its lives, I closed the front door firmly behind me, sliding the chain across and sending up a prayer of thankfulness.

Choices and Consequences

A few months after my lucky escape I was waiting at the top of my street and on the other side of the road. My Mum and sister were to pick me up for the break-up party of our local badminton club. A good-looking guy with a head of curly hair strode out from the house I was standing outside of and with a mischievous grin asked me what I was up to. We chatted for a few minutes before I was picked up and whisked away by mum. Just as I was getting into the car he suggested I might meet him at a local bar the following night for a drink.

It seemed like my luck was changing! By now I knew several people who frequented that bar and felt somewhat confident going there especially with my new friend from work. That next night I saw the mystery guy being served at the bar in front of me and beamed him a smile. He ignored me! Feeling somewhat devastated and disappointed, my friend and I went to the bar, got ourselves some drinks and then went outside to find somewhere to sit.

Suddenly I heard a voice saying, "There she is!" I looked over at a table and was startled to see the mystery guy - and an exact replica who was obviously his twin sitting across from him. The guy who had ignored me at the bar! The tension I had felt at being ignored was forgotten and melted away in an instant when I realized I had made an identity mistake. This had triggered an emotional response which then passed! We sat down, joined in and had a marvelous time.

One of his friends, Russell was caught red-handed smoking a joint by the manager and was banished from the garden bar so went home early. The rest of us laughed and drank and laughed some more and stayed until closing time. Then the twins and my friend and I weaved our way back to my place. Still not understanding how attraction worked and wanting to make him fall in love with me so I could feel connected, I had sex with him. About midway through, I felt violently sick. I untangled myself, rushed to the window and threw up. Every half hour for the next 24 hours I vomited. I couldn't even keep water or an ice cube down.

I went to the doctor and informed him that I either had a horrible virus... or that I might have long term alcohol poisoning. I didn't drink more than usual but I thought I should confess to the Doc that the alcohol might be the problem. He suggested I lay off alcohol for a week to see what happened. The result was startling. I didn't drink for a week and then the following week when I went to the bar I could barely tolerate a couple of glasses of beer. Prior to that it had taken about 8 beers and 4 double whiskeys before I even started to wobble.

However, after the vomiting incident I was well and truly lubricated after only two glasses of beer. Yet I hadn't even reached the legal age to drink! Instead of being concerned about what I was doing to my body, I was thrilled that it had become so cheap to get drunk.

However, mystery man wasn't impressed with my constant drunken state therefore he refrained from advancing our sexual connection into a fully-fledged relationship. And as frequently as I sought sexual intimacy with him, having him as a loving partner in life continued to elude me.

I was smitten by mystery man (Tony) for many months. Unlike the movies which portray love and sex as being synonymous, despite all my efforts it wasn't working out that way for me. His friend Russell was always nice to me although he was much older than I was by over 10 years. After a period of time I stopped chasing Tony because I was somewhat flattered by the fact that finally, someone seemed to genuinely like me for who I was. That someone, was Russell.

Having gone through most of my teen years without a steady boyfriend, when I was 19 I hit the jackpot. As well as Russell being keen on me, I rekindled a friendship with a boy I had known at high school. Vaun had been one of the popular kids and even though we both recognized a feeling of *something* back then, he refrained from asking me out because I wasn't in the popular crowd and he was... *and* he didn't know how to approach me as I was somewhat different from the girls he was used to.

One night, after meeting unexpectedly at another local bar, he and his friend walked with me and my friend back to my place. He admitted that he had a thing for me at school and regretted not getting to know me back then. It seemed like we naturally picked up on the connection we had felt at school, but without the related complications.

I liked both of them, so I dated both of them. Russell and Vaun. It felt like I was coming into my power. At that point in time I didn't understand how attraction worked but I was playing one off against the other. They both felt like they had to compete for my attention and I was so focused on entertaining myself that I just left them to figure it out. After a couple of months of this competitive rivalry, Vaun told me he wanted me to dump Russell and only go out exclusively with him. He said he felt deeply for me and wanted us to become a couple.

I had every intention of breaking up with Russell. We went to a party that Saturday night and the whole time I was trying to figure out a way to break it to him without hurting him. But I couldn't do it. Illogically, I decided in that moment instead to break it off with Vaun and be exclusive with Russell. It was a totally random decision and one that I would later live to regret, sooner rather than later!

I was 19 when I entered into a long-term relationship with Russell. He had just turned 30. With him being considerably older than me, I felt like I was constantly learning from the episodes of his own life experiences. He seemed relaxed and likeable and he was my first boyfriend ever whom my Dad really liked and approved of. This immediately raised his esteem in my eyes.

Unfortunately, my Dad was going through his own challenges at this time in my life. Like me, he had battled negative thoughts and emotions for many years. He and Mum didn't get on so well in the later years of their relationship although they tried. I guess he also felt like he didn't fit in with us. Or so we were soon to discover.

Although they weren't compatible as a couple, they were well-meaning parents and stayed together for the benefit of my sister and me. However, their relationship was constantly strained, and they had many arguments in their attempt to feel heard and understood. None of us had developed effective communication skills and like so many other people making their way through life, we continued to feel disconnected and alone even within a family circle.

Eventually my dad suffered from a mental breakdown. He used to train race horses and an unfortunate error in judgement caused his trainer license to be revoked. Training horses was his absolute passion in life, probably the reason why he had never cultivated either the desire or the skills to build a strong relationship with my Mum, sister and myself. Martyn had been a source of absolute joy for Dad but even Martyn couldn't connect or get through to him at this time.

As much as Mum, Tania and I had craved his love and acceptance, he just didn't understand how to communicate it or to show us his love. Dad had spent a lot of his time down country in the area he had grown up in and he spent a great deal of time there convalescing after his breakdown. One day when he was up visiting with Mum, he calmly told me that without his license to train horses, he had no reason to live.

That comment was upsetting to me every time I thought of it over the next few days. I mulled over it, examined it, depressed myself over it and it caused a great deal of stress and drama between Russell and I - even though I hadn't mentioned it to him verbally. I kept having an uneasy feeling inside myself which led me to react in a hypersensitive manner. A couple of days later, Russell blew up and told me that I didn't need a boyfriend, I needed a father.

Visibly upset due to his comment triggering depressing thoughts after what my Dad had said to me, I fled from the house with tears pouring down my face. When Russell eventually caught up to me I blurted out what Dad had said. With a concerned expression, he then wrapped me in his arms and coaxed me back up to the house. I hadn't told anyone else, I had kept it to myself and the comment and its imagined ramifications were tormenting me endlessly. By the time I finally gained the courage to confront Dad about it he had moved back down country where he was staying with his cousin Lynn.

About two weeks later, Lynn had an uneasy feeling one morning before going to work and said to Dad, "Now, you're not going to do anything silly, are you?" and Dad calmly replied "No."

I was sitting at home with Russell, discussing our day when the phone rang. I picked it up and heard my Mum sobbing, then heard her say, "I can't tell her." My sister took over the phone and told me to sit down. When I had confirmed I was sitting she said, "Dad committed suicide this morning."

Within a few hours of Lynn leaving for work, he had put a gun up to his throat and blown his brains out. I had just turned 20.

I was glad to have Russell there with me as we all drove down country to where Dad's extended family had gathered. I remember us all sitting in a big circle in a large room. Everyone was telling stories about Dad, what a wonderful man he was, how amazing he was with the children, what a peaceful outlook on life he had and what an inspiration he had been to everybody in the community. Mum and Tania and I all looked at each other in bewilderment. Who was this man they were all speaking of? We had rarely experienced Dad behaving in this manner. It was even more disheartening because we were his immediate family and it felt like they were talking about a complete stranger.

At the end of the week we came home to what I perceived would be our new life. I was determined to learn how to feel better about living as Dad's approach to ending it all had shocked me to my core. Although having contemplated suicide many times in my teens, I had never realized the damage that the shock of suicide does to the well-being of everyone else. The blame, the guilt, the recriminations. I knew it was unlikely I could have saved Dad from himself, however, from that experience I knew that I wanted more for myself. I wanted to feel loved. I wanted to feel connected. I wanted to feel like I belonged. And I wanted a fulfilling sex life! I dreamed of a life worth living.

Like so many other young adults who are confused about what is required of them concerning sex, I read magazines and articles, tried different positions and was constantly disappointed when nothing seemed to work, and I couldn't figure out what I was doing wrong. This failure had caused me to be quite promiscuous as a teen, constantly trying to find the answer to my problem.

Although I had several sexual partners in my teen years in my quest to find reciprocating love, it seemed that whenever I engaged in sexual activities, I felt like I was just going through the motions. I would enjoy some parts of it, but my mind was constantly distracted. For the most part, it felt like I was disconnected and isolated from my body.

Due to the emotional and mental damage, I felt I had experienced as a teen, I thought I would never be able to relax and fully enjoy sex. I had lost all confidence in being able to participate fully during sexual intimacy with a partner. I was also worried about my inability to achieve orgasm.

I had reasoned that due to the sexual abuse I had endured as a teen, it had messed up my internal wiring and I was forever doomed to failure. Regardless of the abuse in my past, I desperately wanted to be able to feel fulfilled, to be able to satisfy a partner and to personally achieve orgasms during sex.

Yet, when participating during any sexual activity, I felt anxious, distracted and nervous. I didn't really know what was expected of me. Sex Education in school never teaches teens the advanced knowledge of "how to operate" our vehicles, which is the knowledge we all require to be able to succeed in fully functioning relationships as adults!

As the years passed I began to dread sexual intimacy with Russell because it felt like it always ended up in failure and disappointment for me. I was desperate to have a normal sex life, but it seemed totally out of my reach. It reached the point where I started to avoid being intimate. Even though I loved the attention of kissing and cuddling, when he started to become more passionate I would push him away fearing that he would want me to have sex.

It's interesting to note that everyone else thought we had an amazing relationship. It just goes to show that you never know what's going on behind someone's closed bedroom doors...

My conflicting thoughts, actions and obvious reluctance for sex put a huge strain on our relationship. The thing that I coveted the most – a mutually fulfilling relationship on all levels, just didn't seem like it was ever going to happen. We were best friends and he was my life, but there was no passion in our sex life.

I found myself making excuses as to why I couldn't (or wouldn't) engage sexually. Due to my ongoing lack of interest in sex, Russell eventually developed an erectile dysfunction (weak erection) problem.

It wasn't just the sexual dysfunction which was putting me off sex. Russell had a gambling addiction which he placed above everything else in his life. I had left my job at the photo lab to work with him in his lawn mowing round and a few months later we moved into a rural area on the outskirts of town. The constant strain of him losing money did nothing to make me feel turned on toward him emotionally or sexually.

I had made the mistake of saying yes when he suggested we pool our money together. We were so broke most of the time that our van would constantly run out of fuel. I became a familiar sight to the local residents, with the gas canister in my hand and my thumb turned out so I could pick up a ride to refuel. Russell always insisted that I was the one who went as he thought that people would feel sorry for me because I was a female. So much for gallantry!

None of us knows what's around the next corner. What can start off as a perfectly normal day can quickly deteriorate to become our worst nightmare.

One of our biggest clients was the local bar situated on the outskirts of town. The lawn area was extensive, there was probably about an acre of grass inclusive of the perimeter around the car park as well as the garden bar. Every Monday morning, we would arrive like clockwork at 8:30 am and I would inwardly cringe at the sight of all the rubbish littering the lawns, gardens and parking lot.

Russell and I approached each lawn and gardening job like a well-oiled machine. My job was to prepare the area for the lawn mower. This meant leaping out of the van as soon as we got there and dashing around each property to pick up the offending rubbish as fast as I could. If any rubbish was missed, the lawn mower would shred it into a gazillion pieces and spread them wildly like confetti across the freshly manicured lawn. This was to be avoided at all costs as it doubled my clean up time and then Russell would get grumpy if he was anxious to place bets on upcoming horse races.

While I was picking up rubbish, Russell would attend to fueling up his mower. Since I had to stay ahead of the mower with the line trimmer as well pick up the rubbish, I would always fuel the line trimmer and ensure there was enough line ready for the next lawn at the end of the previous job, so I could just fire it up and go. It was most frustrating if Russell had used the line trimmer after me because he would never replace the line spool or take the time to refuel it for me which inadvertently would put me behind schedule... and make him grumpy!

It was also my job to keep an eye on our dog Jazz. Not long after Dad had died, Russell had arrived home one day with this seriously cute eight-week-old puppy squirming in his arms. We couldn't quite figure out her breed, she appeared to be a cross between a short-haired German Shepherd and some smaller breed. She was light tan in color and of slim medium build.

For most of our jobs Jazz had to stay in the van, however, the new bar owner also had a dog. We decided that because we were there so early, and the bar was for the most part deserted, we would allow them to play unsupervised. Both dogs were about a year old and the two youngsters would tear around the empty carpark and garden bar in a hot pursuit game of tag.

After we had moved out to live in the rural area, we bought a self-drive mower which made Russell's task of mowing big jobs like this country estate so much easier. The problem with that meant I had to be twice as fast to complete my tasks so I could stay ahead of the mower. At this particular job, my first task was to go around the outer lawn surrounding the carpark and pick up all the rubbish, so Russell could start mowing that massive perimeter lawn. Then I'd pick up all the rubbish in the car park. Then I would race around the outer perimeter of the carpark lawn with the line trimmer and also "edge" the grass away from the concrete blocks surrounding the small grass islands which dotted the parking lot.

Putting the line trimmer down, I would then race into the garden bar, pick up the rubbish and then pick up the gazillion cigarette butts that were carelessly tossed by thoughtless drinkers onto the lawn. The mower would shred up any butt that was left behind and the owner liked the garden bar to look meticulous which meant I had to pick up nearly half a bucket of the smelly things. It was so time consuming! I would then dash around the garden bar with the line trimmer to ready it in time for the mower. After Russell finished mowing, I would then sweep the paths clear of grass. It was near impossible to keep an eye on Jazz as well as complete all these tasks on time and a couple of weeks prior I had said to Russell that he needed to share the responsibility of looking out for her.

One fateful morning I was busily picking up the cigarette butts from the garden bar when I heard a screech of tires and a sickening thud followed by an agonized yelp. In a flash, I dropped the bucket and raced around the corner of the historic building. The bar owner's dog, Jess, came careering around the corner with a terrified expression on her face and her tail between her legs. She was visibly shaking as she bolted upstairs to the office.

With my heart in my throat I made it around to the front of the building in record time. There was Jazz, sprawled in a tangled heap on the pavement with most of her intestines hanging out of her torn, bleeding and battered body. Moving more slowly now, a bus full of horrified city commuters continued on down the road. The two young dogs hadn't been paying attention and chased each other across the road. While they had both made it across unscathed, on the way back Jazz was clipped on her side by the passing bus and smashed up onto the sidewalk with the force of it.

She saw me approaching and whimpered weakly. Unbelievably, she was still alive. Her eyes were wide with stark terror and agonized pain. I eased myself down to sit next to her and tenderly cradled her head between my hands. There was nothing I could do but sit with her and offer her the comfort of my presence while a torrential flood of guilty tears blurred my vision and rolled down my cheeks.

After Jess's frantic arrival at her mistress's office, the bar owner came racing downstairs. She had heard the noise too and was relieved when her dog arrived safe and sound. After taking in the scene and confirming Jazz was still alive she raced back upstairs to call the vet to come and put her out of her misery.

Russell was about to find out too. With his earmuffs subduing all noise, he had just finished mowing the grass islands in the parking lot and was on his way to mow the garden bar lawns. He immediately became concerned when he saw the bucket lying on its side with cigarette butts strewn carelessly across the path with no sign of me or Jazz. After running up to the corner he arrived breathlessly but slowed as he approached and surveyed the awful scene. Then he looked at me angrily and contemptuously yelled, "This is all your fault Jacqui! YOU were supposed to be watching her!" I was already devastated for Jazz and my loss and his cruel words would torment me for days. He honestly believed it was my fault. He then walked away and left me to deal with Jazz dying by myself.

It took ten minutes for the vet to arrive. Jazz was still alive, her breathing ragged and hoarse. Her eyes were dull, she was shaking uncontrollably and obviously in horrendous pain. I knew there was no hope for her, her injuries would obviously be fatal. As the vet prepared the injection, I locked my eyes on her and held her gaze. She looked at me trustingly. Even when her eyes glazed over with the light behind them forever extinguished I continued to hold her while I rocked backward and forward, crying. I had stayed strong for her right up to the end, not letting her sense my distress and doing my very best to try to soothe her terror.

The horror wasn't over. Jess's owner gave us a blanket to wrap her up with. With his mouth set in a grimace, Russell picked her up and carried her over to the van. We drove home in silence. More recriminations would come later. When we arrived home, I went to the main house to inform our landlords of the sorry tale. The kind-hearted couple directed us to a small area of garden where their other pets had been lovingly buried.

We began digging her grave. It was the middle of summer and the ground was rock hard. It was like trying to dig through concrete. By the time we thought her final resting ground was big enough, several hours had passed and rigor mortis had set in. We gently lowered her into the grave but her front legs were fully extended and one of her paws was sticking out of the hole. We were mortified, it was like being stuck in some B-grade horror movie. Even though she was dead, we couldn't bring ourselves to break her leg, so it would fit the hastily dug grave. With tears of frustration, fatigue and loss, we pulled her out and dug the hole deeper. Finally, the gut wrenching deed was finished.

Bereft without the lively Jazz, we endured one week in each other's company without a dog. The strained silences were unbearable. But neither of us knew how to deal with our emotions, so we went out and got another dog to fill the void. Russell was insisting that we would call the new dog "Blue" in an odd kind of memorial similarity for "Jazz."

There wasn't the internet back in those days, so we looked through all the advertisements in the newspapers. Russell wanted another Shepherd X like Jazz and we eventually found an ad for some of that breed of puppies who were in need of a new home. It was another long, silent drive there. When we arrived, there were half a dozen gorgeous black and tan puppies milling around. I plonked myself down on the driveway and they promptly started licking me and crawling all over me. I was in puppy heaven!

Russell then said to me, "Which one do you like?" How could I decide? They were all gorgeous. Then he pointed to the far side of the property where a stark white pup was off investigating the area by herself. He said, "I want that one." A white pup? I wanted a Jazz replica. But as usual, Russell got what he wanted.

The pups were near starving and riddled with fleas. This particular pup however, had well and truly landed on her paws. Happily cradling her in my hands we called in at the bar on our way home to show her off and then took her home to pluck off her fleas and feed her. She was all white other than a brindle patch over one eye and another brindle patch over the opposite ear. She gulped greedily at the milk and wolfed down the meat offered. She was such a spunky little pup we didn't have the heart to curse her with the name Blue. And so, we decided on a blend of the two names and called her "BJ".

Unlike Jazz, BJ wasn't big on cuddles. But she had the most uncanny knack of placing herself between me and Russell whenever we argued. She'd just waltz right up and plant herself in the middle of an argument. She would bark at us if we didn't stop. A pure white distraction.

My Dad had trained race horses, but I didn't really know about the gambling aspect of horse racing until

I had met Russell. Russell was totally addicted to gambling. It wasn't until I started doing the lawn mowing round with him that I realized the extent of his addiction.

In between cutting lawns, he would go to the local TAB and place his bets. With the money earned from one lawn, he would invest it in perhaps three races then stop in the middle of mowing the next lawn, so he could listen to the races. This would continue throughout the day and was a great source of frustration and annoyance to me as I couldn't finish work until he returned and finished also.

I would spend half an hour or more sitting in the van outside the TAB waiting for him to finish his gambling fix in between jobs. Other times he would drive away from a job leaving me to complete it and not return until I had finished and had been waiting for over an hour! I wasn't at all impressed with this behavior however, I was needy back in those days, so I allowed his blatant disregard of the value of my time to continue.

Russell was addicted to the adrenaline rush. Of placing the bet on time, of the horses approaching the finishing line. He was addicted to how good it felt when he thought about winning and addicted to the win itself. Part of his related feeling fix was comparing his wins with other gamblers in the bars and TABs in which he frequented.

In time spent with Russell, weekends were the most challenging due to races going off every 10-20 minutes. I had the choice of either going out with him and having to stop every half an hour to an hour at the TABs on the way to and from our destination, or stay home and do my own thing. Unfortunately, for me, our relationship was always a sad threesome. Russell and me and the TAB.

Unfortunately, back then I was mostly reliant on Russell to spend time with me and fulfil me as a person. I would soon tire of whatever I was doing after a few hours and wish that I was with him. Looking at this now, I would have been putting a great deal of pressure on him to fulfil me as a person. This would have triggered frustration and the associated emotional responses within him which he inadvertently suppressed... which would have made him reach for more of his external feeling fixes!

Any need resulting from a suppressed emotional response will result in the vicious cycle of neediness continuing, for all involved.

I would sometimes joke that we only ever went to a bar on days ending with "y". One of these days shocked me to the core of my being. One day I recognized one of Vauns' older brothers sitting at a table near the bar, but he didn't recognize me. I had been curious for many years, about what may have happened to Vaun. Where he was, what he did, how life unfolded for him. If he was happy. Contemplating the life, he may now be living, I asked his brother, who was dating one of the bar staff. His answer was somewhat of a shock.

He looked at me searchingly and hesitated before answering, "Vaun hasn't been doing so well. Several years ago, he got together with this girl... and she broke up with him and chose another man and I don't think he ever got over it. He was crazy about her."

I looked at him, but through him with my thoughts racing. I think my jaw must have dropped in shock and disbelief. In that moment of stunned disbelief, after glancing guiltily behind me at Russell who was placing a bet at the TAB, I briefly contemplated the life I had chosen to live with Russell and how different life might have been if I had chosen to be with Vaun.

Knowing that I was that girl who had broken Vauns' heart, I stammered some sort of incoherent reply, knocked a stool over and bumped into another table in my haste to get away. I saw the flicker of understanding and recognition on his face as he suddenly realized who I was... and ultimately who I had chosen instead of Vaun.

To this day I still think about Vaun from time to time and hope that life is going well for him.

One fateful day, Russell received the news that his father had been diagnosed with cancer. Having always been a vibrant, hearty man, it was distressing to see how quickly he deteriorated. Within two short months he was lying in hospital struggling to take his remaining breaths.

While continuing to attend a Hospice group after he died, Russell's Mum Pat met a lovely man who had lost his wife to cancer also. Their shared humor and belief in the Christian faith led them into a whirlwind romance. A few months later they became engaged and within 6 months they were married. They decided that neither of them were getting any younger and that life was too short to be wasted!

With the intent of moving in with her new husband, Pat asked if Russell and I would move into her house and keep an eye on his younger brother. Martin was twelve years younger than Russell and prone to a nervous disposition. Unlike his brothers whose life experience had taught them to grow up robustly independent, Martin had been sheltered and coddled as a child and therefore hadn't gained the skills to be mentally or emotionally equipped to deal with the pressures of life.

Soon after Russell's father died, and Pat had remarried, Russell and I moved into her home and paid a ridiculously low rent for caring for the house and looking out for Martin. I felt a great deal of resistance towards moving back from the country and back into suburbia. I didn't at all want to share our space with anyone else. However, I conceded to Russell that I was willing to give it two years. Two years, no more! He agreed with me, I'm sure just to pacify me. As a gambler, there was no way he was ever going to miss an opportunity which made it so easy and cheap for him to live!

It was about this time that I developed an interest in organic food, health and natural healing. One of our lawn mowing clients owned a natural health center and one of the therapists who worked there asked us to also mow his lawn. Instead of paying us, we would swap for fortnightly acupuncture sessions. It was he who suggested to me that the best thing I could do for my liver was to give up drinking alcohol. I thought highly of this therapist as a person and I was generally feeling better within myself, so I did, I gave up drinking altogether!

I then started drinking a lot more water and my lifelong asthma disappeared completely. It makes sense because our lungs require half a cup of water a day to function properly and without drinking enough water we don't replenish that need.

Russell and I had both given up smoking ciga-rettes a couple of years earlier. While I hadn't want-ed to stop smoking, Russell insisted that he couldn't give up if I continued smoking in front of him. In order to pacify him while he quit cold turkey, I cut down to five a day for six weeks, then promised to give them up completely at the end of that duration.

I remember that when I gave up smoking ciga-rettes, I would puff on an imaginary cigarette. I'd imagine inhaling the smoke, feeling the deliciousness of the imaginary smoke filling my lungs and then imagine blowing all that smoke out in a long exhalation of breath. It felt like I was participating with the real thing! Albeit it was a much healthier option.

Other than our sex problems, the stress of Russell's gambling addiction and the resistance I felt toward living with his brother, these were the most productive times in my life. I learned how to do energy healing and became quite well known nationally for my ability. I then started overseeing and facilitating healing groups. I had found another feeling fix and it had nothing to do with abusing substances.

When we frequented bars (which due to Russell's gambling addiction was every other day) I began contenting myself by playing games of pool or if there was a dance floor and a band, I would dance.

I delighted in the fact that whereas in the past it had taken me numerous alcoholic drinks to get up and dance, now I would be the first person on the dance floor. Having the floor to myself was wonderful! Toward the end of the night when others were well lubricated, and the floor would become sticky with spilled drinks and packed with drunken, wobbly dancers, I would then remove myself to the pool tables for my other favorite form of entertainment. I was loving the distinct advantage I had when other players started getting drunk and began losing their coordination with their eyesight! For the first time in my life I was loving being sober.

There was one time at the RSA (Returned Servicemen's Association) when I was in such a happy place. Russell and the twins and another friend Phil were filling the room with their lively banter. I felt so in tune, relaxed and happy... and looking forward to being next up on the pool table. Even with my shaking hands I won the first game. I didn't recognize the next player. With the balls racked up by the loser for the next game the new player confidently approached the table and whack! He scattered the balls cleanly across the table. None of the balls had been pocketed, however, so it was now my turn.

I approached the table feeling relaxed and happy then contemplated my first shot and how it would impact the second ball I had in mind. I lined up the white ball to my chosen ball and the pocket, then struck the center of the white ball with my cue. Into the top right pocket, the colored ball went with the white ball lining up perfectly for my next shot. Feeling in alignment with myself I lined up the white ball to the next ball to the pocket, cued the white and into the pocket the ball went. Next ball into the pocket, next ball and the next. I felt like I was in my element. Some of the shots were easy, some weren't. I easily moved from one ball to the next with the white ball positioning almost exactly where I wanted it to each time. The 6th and 7th ball were superb shots and by this time I had garnered the attention of everyone at the nearby tables. They all watched with bated breath.

After pocketing my 7 balls in a row without missing a shot, I finally made it onto the black. My opponent hadn't had another turn since breaking the balls open on the table, so all of his balls were cluttering up the table, in the way of the black. There was only one shot open to me, so I took it, a complicated double off the far side of the table. One of the opponent's balls was sitting right near the pocket I was doubling the black ball into, so I could have just as easily lost the game. But I didn't, I won.

As a loud cheer went up around the room, I shook my opponent's hand and ecstatically walked over to our table, my hands still shaking and my heart racing with excitement. That's when Phil said to me, "Do you know who that guy is? He just came back from winning the National 8 Ball Champs two weeks ago - which means he's now won the Nationals three times and you just down-trou'ed him!"

My opponent then came over to me and asked what I wanted to drink, then said, "That was incredibly played. Well done. I don't know how a person's hands can shake so much and still place such great shots! We've just got to have another game later, so I know it wasn't a fluke."

When it was time to approach the table for our next game, my heart was hammering nervously. I tried to control the shaking in my hands, but it wouldn't stop, it was getting worse by the moment. Suddenly I wasn't just playing for my enjoyment of playing the game, I was playing to prove myself. All the old doubts from my past surfaced, I was hyper aware of my shaking and soon my whole body began trembling uncontrollably.

I couldn't focus and was distracted knowing that everyone was now watching me. I wasn't feeling at all relaxed and at ease this time, my first available shot was an easy one and I missed. When I walked away from the table my legs seemed to be weighed down with lead. I was so disappointed. My opponent began to confidently clean up the table as I had in our previous game. I was relieved when he finally missed, and I sunk a ball before he sunk the black - I had worried that this time, *I* would be totally humiliated by facing a "down-trousers"!

Isn't it interesting how we can screw up a game or a task when we perceive that the stakes are higher, and we start judging our own ability?

I enjoyed myself when I was doing things which fulfilled me although I didn't really have much in the way of hobbies back in those days. And for the first eight years of my relationship with Russell I didn't drive a vehicle either. This caused many an argument after I stopped drinking, due to Russell still being a drinker and my unwillingness to take up the mantle of being the sober driver.

Russell was known as the life of most parties and would want to stay to the bitter end. He had a talent as a DJ, to find the right music and delighted in receiving compliments for his obvious skill. For me, especially after I stopped drinking alcohol, this need for him to be the last man standing became tedious over the years. I felt that I was growing as a person and he was still stuck in a rut. I often worried about his ability to drive in various states of inebriation and found it difficult to trust that he would remain coherent enough to get us home safely.

I had tried numerous techniques and visualizations to try and get over my fear of driving and very slowly over many years I began to feel somewhat less intimidated. Fatefully, one night I was unexpectedly thrown into the driver's seat. Russell and I had been at a bar for several hours and he became too drunk to drive. He had also spent all our money, so we couldn't afford a taxi. I had a client booked in for an early start so staying there locally at a friend's place was also out of the question.

With my heart wildly hammering and my head feeling like it was stuffed full of cotton wool, I sat at the steering wheel waiting for him to finish saying his goodbyes. He was drunk, so this took quite some time! I just sat there in the driver's seat waiting for him with the engine running. My legs were shaking uncontrollably, my feet poised above the accelerator and clutch.

Although I didn't realize it at the time, I was actually allowing the physical discomfort of the emotional response to be felt. I didn't try to make it go away. I just sat there in total discomfort waiting for him to get organized, so we could go.

He finally got into the car. I took a slow, shaky breath and moved the manual stick into first gear. I continued to breathe slowly and carefully applied some acceleration. I maneuvered out of the parking lot and onto the main highway steadily applying the accelerator as I shifted through the gears.

About mid-way home I suddenly realized that I was enjoying myself! I was actually enjoying driving! I made it all the way home without incident and have been happily driving ever since. (The following weeks after I realized I could drive incident free, he would complain because I always had the car out!)

We had several commercial properties in our lawn mowing and gardening business and one of these included a large market garden with a café. The owner, Peter, was incredibly difficult to get along with. He was abrupt, rude and highly critical. One sunny morning we rolled up to cut his lawns. Russell made a sarcastic comment about what a horrible person Peter was to deal with. However, next to the local bar it was our highest paying lawn - and like the bar it was weekly, which made it feel like gold.

Personally, I had been contemplating a new strategy to try and break through Peter's stern demeanor.

With my newfound understanding and awareness of energy and healing, I figured there must be some good in everyone. I was determined to see it in Peter. Therefore, every time I thought of interacting with him, instead of denying those intense resistant related feelings when they surfaced, I stopped fighting them. Within moments I would feel more calm and relaxed when thinking about him.

On this morning, I was contemplating an imagined happy interaction with Peter as I went around the property, trimming the grass back from the trees and edges. I wasn't far from finishing, when I saw Peter striding toward me.

My heart was pounding wildly as I removed my earmuffs. I looked him in the eye and waited, with heart pounding, half expecting him to chew me out over some minor issue. I could hardly believe my ears when he said to me, "Jacqui, I just came over to say what a great job you do. Thank you so much for all your hard work, I really appreciate it."

You can imagine how excited I was at the thought of reporting this to Russell! When I got back to the van however, Russell was doggedly pushing his lawn mower across the driveway, his face bright red and set in a grim expression. Before I could open my mouth, he said to me, "I can't believe what that prick Peter did! I was mowing the café lawns and he said to me, "When was the last time you changed your blades? You're not doing a very good job!"

I was stunned (and figured that sharing my own exciting encounter at this time was not such a good idea.) I asked what time he had said that, and it was before Peter had spoken to me. Figuring that his mood had sweetened after offloading on Russell, I went into the shop to get paid. I heard Peter loudly and angrily reprimanding several staff members on his way to the counter.

Then, low and behold when he saw me, a big smile lit up his face. "Jacqui, let me get some cash together for you. Great job you did today." He then turned to one of his staff members and rudely barked an order at them. *That* was interesting! It felt like I was onto something.

Over the next couple of months, I continued to test this theory with Peter. Some weeks I wasn't in such a relaxed emotional state and would stubbornly resist my emotional responses when they were triggered. Doing demanding physical work in the hot sun, they were triggered often!

It's interesting to note that at the times when I, myself was being resistant to any thoughts occupying my mind, Peter would always be difficult to deal with. Yet, the times I allowed my triggered emotional resistance by not fighting it or trying to make it go away, Peter had no problems with me. It was like he was a completely different person.

He would switch between a Jekyll and Hyde personality depending on who was acting resistant toward him. Most of his staff expected him to be a grumpy prick and to them, he usually was. On the other hand, Peter was totally devoted to his wife and children and they rarely experienced him being gruff and short tempered.

Life is always giving us lessons. One of Martin's friends Kerry, had become a more than regular visitor at our house. Russell liked to pick his brains and nurture his friendship because he was a lawn mower mechanic. Kerry was for the most part a loner, quiet, considerate and thoughtful, a studious man with a gentle nature. I really liked him, however he would come over to our place EVERY single day. Not to share anything, just to be there so he didn't have to sit alone with his thoughts.

Every day he would arrive on our doorstep, stay for about 4 or 5 hours and then go home. He generally didn't talk much, would mostly listen to music, smoke pot and engage with Russell and Martin in the man cave (the shed.) He rarely spoke about his problems other than mentioning some tension he was experiencing at home and at work.

After a year or so of him *always* being at our place, we were starting to feel like we weren't having enough time to ourselves. We'd hear a car in the driveway and one of us would glance out the window and say, "Oh, it's Kerry," with no enthusiasm at all. He had become a constant drain on our energy and his never-ending visits were making us feel somewhat smothered.

It got to the point where it became unbearable. One day I told Russell we had to do something about it. To save our sanity, we would have to say something to Kerry. In true Russell fashion, he insisted that I be the one to say something. The next day I said to Kerry as he was leaving, "We really like and appreciate you as a person Kerry, however, Russell and I need some more time for ourselves as a couple. Would you mind reducing your visits to just a few times a week?" He looked momentarily stunned then his face became devoid of expression, followed by his head and shoulders slumping in disappointment.

Looking back now I can see how important a feeling fix our company had become for him. We had become a point of connection, a distraction from his constant inner turmoil. Unfortunately, he had his mind fixated on his preferred feeling fix and when that was suddenly reduced in frequency he felt alone, overwhelmed and bereft. Two months later we received a phone call from his distressed mother... Kerry had committed suicide.

It was stunning how many people turned up for his funeral. A massive funeral parlor room packed wall to wall with people. Kerry had been unaware of how many people cared for him. For those who arrived late, there was only standing room, even then some were spilling out into the foyer.

Because he didn't know how to deal with the negative thoughts and emotions which were constantly tormenting him, the associated resistance prevented him from reaching out and clearly communicating his needs to anyone. He died because of this lack of knowledge.

It's important to note that when we're in a state of emotional resistance, we can't clearly communicate. It's like we're dialing in between two radio stations and only experiencing the static. Due to the mental confusion this causes, we can't find the words which would clearly express our needs so no one knows or understands the extent of our feeling of disconnection.

A couple of years later when another of Martin's friends became an imposition on our time by constantly visiting as Kerry previously did, Russell flatly refused for either of us to tell him we needed our own space as a couple. Upon querying him as to why, he said, "Look what happened last time we did that!" I couldn't argue his logic so refrained from commenting further. At that time, I did not know that I would become one of those emotionally needy people in the future...

Although Russell rarely cleaned up his own thoughts and actions, one of his redeeming actions was to keep our neighborhood and everywhere else we went clear of rubbish. He always kept an empty sack in the back of the car as well as the work van. After waiting for him to finally vacate a TAB I would then often have to wait in frustration as he insisted on cleaning up the streets on the way to our next location. Whenever he spotted a pile of rubbish cluttering up the gutter he would quickly pull over and whip out his ever-ready canvas sack. He'd then walk the length of the street and back, before heaving the newly-filled rubbish bag into the back of the vehicle.

Unfortunately, he wasn't as dedicated to emptying the bags as he was to be filling them! Many times, I would get in the car and an all-pervading stench of rubbish had filled the car because he had forgotten to remove the rubbish bag. Often, I would suggest he remove the bag as soon as we arrived home and he would say that he'd do it later. Then he would forget. It drove me crazy! I liked my personal space to be clean so instead of viewing his frequent street clearing as the valuable service to society it was, his blatant disregard for my preference became another source of contention and resistance.

Never assume that because someone has only mentioned something once or twice to you out loud, it isn't important. Most people will systematically think about and analyze a problematic subject about a hundred times before verbally mentioning their request.

It's interesting how many times as a species, we will adamantly argue how often we have mentioned something when we have only had that conversation a gazillion times with ourselves. This is what causes a great deal of friction and emotional resistance as both individuals fight to protect their stance and defend their right to feel heard and understood.

Luckily for me, Russell loved to vacuum the house. One of his previous jobs had been as a commercial cleaner and he loved getting that vacuum hose into every nook and cranny. Our youngest dog Zodie also had a passion for vacuum cleaners. Sometimes Russell could barely get the vacuum cleaner out of the cupboard without her pouncing on it. With the powerful noise of the super sucky engine starting up she must have thought the vacuum cleaner was a live beast and would growl and repeatedly pounce on the cleaning head as he attempted to suck the floors clean. It got to the point where he would shut her outside, so he could finish vacuuming uninterrupted.

BJ would also hang around for a different reason - because she herself loved to be vacuumed. She would stand there waiting in anticipation for one of us to pull out the smaller handheld vacuuming device and run it up and down her back while she stood there quivering in the deliciousness of it. Whenever we made any attempt to stop her "preferred method of grooming" she would look around as if to say, "Don't stop now, I'm enjoying this!" BJ had long white hairs which stuck to everything and Russell would vacuum daily. This was a redeeming quality of his that I loved as I personally hated vacuuming.

After several frustrating years of working the lawn mowing business with Russell, I left to work part time elsewhere, so I could have more control over my day. However, I made the mistake of giving Russell my share of the rent money to give to his Mum when he went to mow her lawns.

He would tell her that he needed X amount of dollars to fix something at the house and she would suggest he use the rent money... and he would lose it. Then he would say he needed more... and she would give it and he would promptly lose it. This was an ongoing saga like a soap opera. He sold everything of any value that he could find on the property and have a great time gambling until he eventually lost it all. Then he would be depressed and miserable.

I didn't know that for six months when his mother was living with her second husband, he had not paid her *any* rent money! I was horrified when one day she visited and asked me what was happening with the rent. I asked what she meant, and she replied that it hadn't been paid for six months. I'm sure her distressed and disheartened expression mirrored my own as we both contemplated where it had gone. I was mortified.

Sometimes Russell would win and be ecstatically cheerful, however most of the time he would lose. It was like being on a never-ending rollercoaster ride, never knowing whether he was going to be up or down, which was a little like our sex life. His resulting behavior affected everyone around him.

When he lost several bets in a row he would become sullen. Or irritable. Or angry. If he lost all his earnings in one day, he would become depressed and withdrawn for over a week. He was like a primed hand grenade waiting to explode. The happiness of his day was down to the equivalent of a roll of the dice. There are so many emotional responses which are triggered during an addiction cycle, which affect all involved.

For many years, Russell's gambling addiction put a massive strain on our relationship, both emotionally and financially. He would lie, cheat and make excuses as to why he couldn't pay his share of the bills or for why he was so depressed. But he never took corrective action because he was addicted to the adrenaline rush he associated with gambling. When he sunk into the depths of his own self-induced depression it was like walking on broken glass around him.

After Pat's second husband went into aged care due to advancing Parkinson's disease, she ran into some issues with his family. They insisted they had to rent out his house to pay for his ongoing care. He had plenty of money saved, however, they didn't want their inheritance spent on his care! Their nasty and demeaning attitude toward Pat made her life a misery and difficult for her to continue living there.

When it seemed, there was no avenue for resolution and it was obvious the ongoing worry and stress were taking a toll on her, we somewhat reluctantly asked her to come back home to live with us. For several years I had tried on many occasions to convince Russell to move into our own place out in the country, but he always made excuses.

His gambling continued. On the days when his losses were high, and he was a miserable pain in the proverbial to live with, his Mum and I would bribe him to try and coax him out of his shell. Otherwise his depressed state would feel like a heavy wet blanket which constantly weighted down the whole household, negatively affecting all of us.

I see now that I continued to feed his addiction because I felt sorry for him. I would offer him $20 of my own hard-earned money several times a week to give my shoulders a rub. It's amazing the depths of degradation we will sink to in order to placate a person's addiction because we love them, and we want them to feel better.

But I also had an ulterior motive. I wanted him to stop being so attached to the couch and feeling sorry for himself, so we could go out together and have a life! And if it cost me money to do that, then that's what I decided I had to do.

*We often feed someone else's addiction so we ourselves
don't lose something we perceive ourselves to need.*

Similar to allowing the sexual abuse to continue
in the past because of my need to earn money, now I
was allowing Russell's addiction and his related emotional neglect in our relationship so that I could continue to have my own needs met.

After a big loss, he would stay away from gambling for a day or two, but the need was always bigger than the regret. Needs must be fulfilled one way
or another and gambling provided him with the biggest emotional crutch of all. He just had to have it.

It's likely his need for the gambling fix was a substitute for his inability to feel fulfilled sexually as a
man. The longer the sexual dysfunction problems
went on, the more intense his need for fulfilment via
gambling. He constantly felt a compulsive need to
feel better as our intimate relationship was a source
of constant stress. There was no chance for him to
feel better there!

After 12 incessant years of this constant battle of
win/lose/depression/loss I felt like I couldn't take it
anymore. Losing all his holiday money on the first
day of our autumn holiday was the final straw. I was
completely fed up with rescuing him from what I
then perceived to be his own stupidity. Many times,
over the years I had thought of leaving him, however
I also had it easy living there. As much as I hated the
gambling and the destructive emotional upheaval, I

liked the thought of being totally responsible for myself even less.

However, I could no longer endure the stress associated with the gambling. My stomach would churn into knots when bills arrived and sat on the table well past the due-by date while we waited for his promised share. He had borrowed money from his Mum to buy his work van and I worried that he wasn't paying her back. Whenever I tried to say anything and approach the problem head-on, he would snap at me and accuse me of not trusting him. It was heart-wrenching and soul destroying to live life constantly on the edge of a reactive volcano.

I told him I was walking away, and he begged me to stay. He told me I was the best thing that had ever happened to him, that he couldn't bear the thought of losing me. I told him the associated stress from his gambling addiction was tearing me apart, he had been losing me for years.

Like so many others with an addiction, he promised he would give it up. Pleading with me, with tears in his eyes, he promised to reform. And I foolishly wanted to believe in the better person I could see in him, so I decided to give him one last chance.

It lasted for about six months. Then the inconsistencies returned in his timing and his behavior. Because he hadn't dealt with the emotional aspect of his addiction (or his sex problems) he continued to be needy. During this time of gambling abstinence, he drank more alcohol. He smoked more pot, then would drink more and became obnoxiously drunk. I had swapped one version of hell for another. Once more, he became grumpy and uncommunicative.

His eyes would light up when his friends spoke of gambling. It was obvious he was missing this; his biggest feeling fix of all. I was driving past the mall one day and had a funny feeling in my gut. Going with the feeling, I popped across to the local tavern which had a TAB and saw his van parked out the front. I hesitated to go in and check up on him, after all, hadn't he asked me to trust him? I stepped back and forth and procrastinated for a few minutes in total indecision, then went inside.

There he was, sitting at a table with a betting slip in one hand and a pen in another, riveted to the TV monitor in front of him. Then he saw me. He had the audacity to say he had been contemplating having a bet but hadn't actually placed one! Because there was no proof, what could I do? I gave him the benefit of the doubt. I stayed with him because I saw his potential and I didn't want to give up on that.

I hadn't given up hope for restoring our sex life either. I knew there had to be an answer. Every now and then I would read an article or hear about a new technique which I would immediately want to try out in bed. But to my disappointment, none of them worked for me and I would again experience the fear that I'd never be able to feel fulfilled sexually.

After several years and numerous attempts, the ongoing disappointment destroyed my libido until it just about withered away to nothing. It was no wonder that Russell experienced weak erection problems! My random bouts of appearing attracted and horny, then not, must have been totally messing with his brain! How could he consistently orchestrate a timed erection when I was constantly giving him mixed messages? Unfortunately, sex was no fun for either of us.

Then an event which would truly define my life's purpose, suddenly appeared.

Shock, Expectation and Confusion

One late sunny afternoon I was sitting at the kitchen table reading an article in a woman's magazine about how many women don't allow themselves to enjoy sex. I thought: This is it! *This* is why I haven't been able to orgasm! I haven't been *allowing myself to enjoy* sex. It seemed like the most obvious answer.

I wore a cheeky smile on my face for the rest of the afternoon, gleefully anticipating the evening activities and what might finally happen. We had visitors that night and after they left, Russell came into the room which I used as an office, sat down and said the strangest thing. He said to me, "You know what? I think I've done everything I came here to do." Other than thinking it was a weird comment at the time, I thought nothing more of it.

That night, I actively participated in our lovemaking. I did my best to relax and to enjoy being close to him. Although I didn't achieve an orgasm it was nice to feel like we were connecting, and I could sense Russell's appreciation of my effort. I thought to myself, "This is just the start!"

I woke the next morning feeling happy and excited. I noticed his side of the bed was empty but thought nothing of it as he would often go into another room if he couldn't sleep so he wouldn't disturb me. With a sly grin, I dashed into the bathroom to clean my teeth and freshen my breath in readiness to pounce on him and continue where we had left off the night before.

He was sitting on the sofa, positioned upright with eyes closed and a peaceful expression on his face. It seemed wrong to wake him, so I grabbed a blanket, figuring he would probably be cold. As I shook out the blanket I accidentally bashed him in the face with my elbow. His head just lolled to the side. I looked at him in horror, all my dreams smashing into a million pieces.

I couldn't believe it. NO WAY! I put my hands on each of his shoulders and started shaking him. "Russell, wake up!" No answer. I couldn't believe it - his timing was terrible. Not when I thought I had found the answer to our sex problems! I slowly shook him again, trying to *will* him into waking up, saying in time with each shake of his shoulders, "THIS.. IS.. NOT.. PART.. OF.. THE.. PLAN!" but his head just lolled loosely from side to side with each word stated. There was no other movement, not even a twitch of a muscle. Absolutely nothing. He was most certainly cold - and had been for several hours.

While all I wanted to do was sit there in stunned disbelief I knew I had to become the responsible one. I started making up a mental checklist. Dial the emergency departments and report a death. Wake Pat up and break the news that her son had died. OH MY GOD, I've got to tell Pat her oldest son is dead! And then I've got to tell Martin. And then I've got to call his other brother and there's a hundred million other phone calls I have to make. None of this was at all appealing to me.

I started with the emergency number, 111. "111, please state your emergency," came the calm voice on the other side of the line. "I need to report a death," I said, "I just woke up and found my partner sitting upright on the sofa, dead."

"Do you know how to do CPR?" asked the voice on the other end.

"Which part of dead don't you understand?" I cried out. "His body is icy cold!"

"Do you know how to do CPR?" that annoyingly calm voice asked me again. "Please do CPR until the ambulance arrives. The ambulance is on its way."

Knowing he was dead and despairing of that fact, I moved the coffee table out of the way and tried to drag Russell onto the floor, so I could perform the CPR and mouth to mouth resuscitation which I had learned so many years ago. However, it was in that moment I learned the true meaning of "dead weight." Trying to maneuver my dead partner from an upright sitting position to lying on his back on the floor of the small room was nearly impossible. He was like a rag doll! I hadn't moved the coffee table far enough out of the way and we kept getting tangled up with it. It was tearing me apart inside to be tripping over his limp dead body parts. Nearing the end of my physical strength and my emotional tether, I finally got hold of him in a more balanced state and staggered onto a small area of vacant floor.

The instructions drummed into me from my life-saving course poured into my mind. Push down on his chest: one, two, three, four, five then check for breath. Cup under his neck, tilt his head back, pinch his nose and breathe into his mouth. Again, push down on his chest: one, two, three, four, five then pause and check for breathing. I followed the learned sequence which seemed to be embedded into my brain. Pushing down on his chest, then pinching his nose and breathing into his mouth. Knowing the whole time that it wasn't going to make a difference. Knowing it was futile, knowing that he was dead. Feeling angry toward the emergency department officer for making me go through this additional torture.

It felt like a lifetime before the ambulance finally arrived. With relief, I shakily stood up and staggered toward the door, my legs weak and tingling from kneeling with my legs bent in the same position for too long. I lead the ambulance officers into the room where Russell was lying so infinitely and uncharacteristically still. They asked me to stand back so they could shock him with a defibrillator to try and restart his heart. On the second attempt the officer started aback, as if there was suddenly hope. But a minute later, he glanced up and said, "Sorry love, he's dead." By this stage, the police had also arrived.

I went and let our dogs out of our bedroom, so they could say their own goodbyes. The youngest, Xena, a two-year-old Staffordshire X who had eventually replaced Zodie, barely acknowledged Russell before bounding outside to play ball with the police officers. BJ, however, was devastated. I was sitting in the lounge chair nearest the door when she entered the room and lowered her nose to cautiously sniff at Russell. On touching his cold skin with her nose, she leapt back in shock with a soft whimper and raced back into the bedroom where she lay in her basket shaking, a forlorn expression on her usually perky white face. Russell had been her best friend for close to 14 years and like me, she was devastated at her sudden loss.

Task one (and two, the dogs) appeared to be completed. Now for the additional drama of informing Pat. Although a woman from Victim Support had arrived and offered to break the sad news to the other family members, I felt it was my responsibility and the very least I could do for all of them. As much as we all drove each other crazy, they had become my extended family.

With a heavy heart, I made the long trek down the hallway to Pat's room. Being quite deaf, she didn't hear me knock on her bedroom door. I turned the handle of the door and eased my way inside, careful not to trip over anything in her crowded room and inadvertently land on top of her. She was curled up into the fetal position facing the wall. I put my hand on her shoulder. "Pat, wake up!" It took a few attempts before she sleepily opened her eyes and a few more seconds before her eyes came into focus enough to see the shocked expression on my face. "What's wrong?" she asked. "Jacqui, what's wrong??"

"It's Russell," I choked back a sob. "He's dead." "Oh no," she said, "No, no, no, no, NO!" The woman from victim support sat with Pat while I went in search of Martin.

I made my way out to Martin's caravan which was adjacent to the house and tentatively knocked on his door. He opened it almost immediately. When I broke the sad news about his brother, he was stunned... he thought something had happened to his mother. It took a few minutes before the fact registered that his vibrant, bossy, oldest brother would no longer be there to guide him and torment him and be his best friend.

Then I had to track down his other brother. Then my Mum and sister, then my boss to tell her I wouldn't be into work for a few days. I rang the twins, Tony and Chris, tried to get hold of our other closest friends including Mark and Ange, then started making a long list of Russell's customers to call.

Russell was dead. No one could believe it. Just four days before his 45th birthday and the night before our 15th anniversary.

Mark and Ange called in. We had all been friends for a really long time and they shared the same anniversary. They became a couple at Russell's 30th which was the same night Russell and I first hooked up as a couple. I remember it had felt weird sitting on the couch the next day holding his hand as a girlfriend when we had spent the first few months just being friends. He had been such a big part of my life and now he was gone. *What was totally shocking was that the coroner couldn't find anything wrong with him.*

We were all stunned. Friends, family – everyone who knew him or knew of him. That fateful day reminded us all that life can be dramatically cut short and that there's no time to waste in feeling unfulfilled. I felt like I had wasted so much time in my life. Time that like Russell, I might not have.

I was devastated. Although our relationship had been a turbulent ride due to our sex problems and

Russell's gambling addiction, we were best friends and he had been my life.

The day of his funeral dawned bright and sunny. It still didn't feel like he was dead, I had imagined that I had felt him with me as I planned the details of his funeral. Because of his love of being outside and the fact that it was in the middle of summer, I requested of the funeral director that we hold the service outside. This had not been done before. We eventually found a lovely spot at the bottom of a hilly knoll with the surrounding high ground making it seem like a natural amphitheater. This seemed to be the perfect location to say our final goodbyes, with a flat area at the bottom, a gorgeous stand of trees behind and plenty of sitting space on the grass.

Guests started arriving. I was surprised at the number of people who turned up to pay their respects, there must have been a hundred people there! Then the funeral director called an issue to my attention. Due to their funeral services, never having been conducted at an outside location, it hadn't occurred to any of us that Russell's casket was on a trolley. This would usually easily be wheeled into the funeral home. But because we were holding the service at the bottom of the somewhat bumpy grass knoll, we would need to have the casket carried to the bottom.

Not thinking clearly, I called for the nearest six men to carry the casket down the hill. Martin and five friends rushed to assist. Unfortunately, Russell's other brother arrived late and missed the opportunity to help carry his brother down. I just wasn't thinking clearly and my resistance to the fact that I was about to say farewell to my best friend diluted my ability to think caringly and rationally.

Did I mention that Russell had a deliciously wicked sense of humor? He certainly had the last laugh that day. He had been a great fan of Johnny Cash, so I had grabbed a compiled CD of Russell's favorite mix of his songs to play while guests were turning up and we were waiting for the service to begin.

As his brother and friends solemnly picked up Russell's casket to carry him to the bottom of the hill, I dashed over to the battery-operated stereo and pressed play. Soon after, Johnny Cash's clear, loud voice echoed around our outdoor auditorium, "I fell into a burning ring of fire. I went down, down, down and the flames went higher. And it burns, burns, burns..." that was about as far as he got before I was able to hastily turn it off! Yes, Russell always insisted on having the last laugh too!

Interestingly, the week before he died, people were randomly turning up to our house and reconnecting. Friends that we hadn't seen for years. Friends whom Russell had fallen out of friendship with. Due to his hyper-sensitivity, whether it was exasperated by his gambling addiction or sexual dysfunctions, Russell would easily take offence at what people said especially while he was drinking. Sometimes I would be in the same room with him, and clearly hear what was nothing more than an innocent observation communicated in a totally non-threatening way.

But when Russell had been drinking and was in one of his sensitive states you would have thought he had been accused of murder. He would become indignant and judgmental and hotly dispute what had been said. Of course, the other person would look on in confusion as Russell tore them to shreds with his unwarranted accusations. He would then flatly refuse to have anything to do with that person and would insist that if I loved him, I wouldn't have anything to do with them either. This was soul destroying and something which I deeply regretted agreeing to allow.

He would refuse contact for several months and sometimes years and some of those friends had become dear and close friends to me. It was like another form of roulette, how long a friend would last before they upset his lordship. Allowing this had been one of those things which made me question why I stayed with him and would constantly eat away at me over our years together.

However, in the week before he died, he seemed to really grow as a person. He had made a decision the previous month to stop gambling once and for all. We were happier than we had ever been. And more than five people whom he hadn't spoken to in up to seven years, randomly got in contact or visited. Russell easily made peace with all of them. It was as though they all *knew*.

The after-funeral party was interesting. Many people were devastated, yet I was on this weird sort of high. I hadn't altogether acknowledged the fact that Russell was dead. Because I could feel his presence so strongly around me, it didn't really feel like he was gone. That was until several hours later, after the party when everyone had left. I cleared away all the empty bottles and overflowing ashtrays and walked up the stairs into the house, then down to the bedroom. Our room. It suddenly seemed void and empty without his vibrant laughter.

BJ was lying in her basket with a forlorn expression on her face. Like Russell, she had always been a party animal, thriving in the presence of others. But without Russell she appeared lost and not knowing what to do with herself. She lay in her basket observing my every move, waiting for me to take charge. That's when reality and the wall of emotion hit me. With a wail of anguish, the tears started flowing. It seemed like they would never stop. It felt like my gut was wrenching apart and I lay sobbing uncontrollably, curled up next to BJ in her basket, sharing that moment of utter desolation with her.

Our house was full of flowers. Some helpful advice when giving flowers, whether in commiseration of mourning or to celebrate a happy event, please present them in a vase. It's inordinately odd how stressful it is when flowers upon flowers upon flowers keep arriving, with nowhere to put them.

The refrigerator was overflowing with meals and snacks and thoughtful contributions. Myself, who had never faltered at the thought of food, suddenly found it near impossible to eat. It was like there was a massive knot in my chest which I had to force the food past. I thought I was going to drown in the intensity of my emotions and related resistance I had toward feeling them. No matter what technique I tried, that lump of overwhelming despair was going nowhere.

Even in his death, Russell's carelessness and lack of attention to detail was putting pressure on me.

In true Russell style he had set no structure for running his business. There were no complete lists of customers or their addresses! Just random bits of information to decipher, scattered throughout the house and his work van. Mark had offered to take on his lawn mowing round and pay me a percentage of sales. It took several weeks to piece together any semblance of a fully functioning operational procedure, and many customers were lost in the process.

The extent of Russell's outstanding debts was only revealed after he died. In my pride, I took responsibility for repaying most of those debts even though they were not mine and Russell and I had never married. Pat helpfully donated Russell's work van to me. Though he had stopped making repayments to her well over a year prior, she continued to be a thoughtful, kind-hearted and considerate woman.

Two weeks after Russell's funeral and after discussing my situation at great length, a friend made a somewhat unusual suggestion... She said that if by chance, I had ever experienced any sexual abuse in the past that I could access fully funded government support for 12 sessions of counselling... that it might help me to overcome my grief.

I jumped at the chance as I felt so alone without Russell. I had always been a spontaneous type of person but everyone else seemed to plan their weekends four weeks in advance. Days would stretch out unbearably and there were way too many hours in a day to fill all by myself.

I wanted to be able to relax but I always felt like there was something I needed to do so I could feel better. The alternative was being swamped by a flood of thoughts from the past which would frequently make me feel alone, isolated and over-whelmed. I just didn't know how to relax and enjoy being me. Everywhere I went, I saw couples walking hand in hand, laughing together, eating together. Everyone else seemed to have someone to be to-gether with, but not me. I was alone again, back to being on the outside of life looking in.

Desperate for answers, I signed up for the free counselling. I remember the look of surprised consternation on the psychologist's face when I admitted the sexual abuse had happened weekly for nearly a year. He had assumed it had only occurred once.

I was so needy of someone to make me feel better, it hurt. Every week I would go to my "talk therapy" session with the psychologist but it never got me anywhere. I still didn't know how to live with myself, how to stop feeling overwhelmed by my emotions. I still felt totally needy and I still hadn't figured out how to enjoy being human.

St Patrick's day was particularly difficult. It was just 4 weeks after Russell died. He had always made a big deal out of what he fondly called "St Pat's Day" and would ensure we were in a bar or at a party dressed in at least one item of green. He would put on his best Irish voice and tell bad Irish jokes until everyone was figuratively (and literally if they had been smoking pot) rolling on the floor laughing.

It was my first St Pat's day as an adult without him. I drifted between various bars which we used to visit and couldn't find anyone we previously hung out with. I sat in the car with tears pouring down my face, feeling completely desolate and alone. As hard as I tried, I just couldn't bring myself to join in with strangers and become part of the local festivities.

With a heavy heart, I finally called the twins as I was feeling desperately lonely. In recent weeks, I had spent a great deal of time at their house. However, I felt that my constant presence there since

Russell died was probably starting to be unwelcome. Always thoughtful and concerned for my well-being, they said yes of course I could come over. When I arrived, I was surprised to find our friend Paul C was staying with them. I had known Paul for years, we had been at primary school together. He had moved up north several years ago and it was always an unexpected delight to see him. He would spend many a night strumming his guitar and entertaining us with classic rock songs and haunting melodies.

The twin's flat mate Phil, was also there. I had always felt a bit of a flutter in my heart when Phil was around even when I was with Russell. He was always kind, humorous and thoughtful. He had his own business and with the entrepreneurial streak which runs in my family, I had always delighted in discussing business strategies with him.

On this particular night, however, business was far from my mind. It was such a relief to fall into their easy banter and sit on the last remaining stool at the breakfast bar while they cooked up a storm. As well as sharing my love for playing 8 ball and snooker they all had a passion for watching cooking shows and trying to outdo each other in the kitchen. This made for many great occasions of taste testing as they competed for the best feedback on their creations.

As I started relaxing and enjoying myself, I wanted the night to go on forever. It had seemed such a long time for my laughter to come easily. However, with the next day a work day, the inevitable close to the evening came. Phil was first and said, "Right, that's me. I'm off to bed." Feeling the butterflies leap out of my chest, I looked at him imploringly and could hardly believe I actually mustered up the courage to say, "Can I come with you? ... I just want to be held tonight..."

He looked at me searchingly for a moment then said, "Sure." And gently he took my hand and led me to his bedroom. As we lay in bed with him holding me and stroking my hair he said, "How come I get to be so lucky?" I turned my head up toward him and answered with a long-awaited kiss.

Phil had many redeeming qualities, one of which was his forthrightness with his young daughter. At just two and a half years old, he didn't baby her or talk in that silly voice which many adults use when talking to small children. He would always speak in a matter of fact voice and deal with any issues in the moment they arose instead of trying to shield and protect her from them.

My white dog BJ had become increasingly grumpy since Russell had passed. It was as though she had lost her enthusiasm for life. Whereas in the past she had always delighted in interacting with small children, kittens, puppies and any other creature who was young of age, she became increasingly impatient and intolerant toward them.

One evening when we were all gathered at the twin's place, Phil's daughter approached BJ from the side and BJ turned around and snapped at her. Imogen cried out in fright and ran to her dad, saying that the dog had tried to bite her. Phil picked her up calmly and said, "Did doggie snap at you? She's an old dog and you just gave her a fright. Come on, let's go over and apologize to her."

With Imogen perched on his hip they slowly approached BJ, who was standing in the middle of the room looking somewhat guilty for having lost her temper. As they neared her, Imogen squirmed a little bit in Phil's arms because she was still feeling fearful and wasn't quite sure what BJ's reception would be. Phil gently but firmly took hold of her hand and together they reached out and stroked BJ down the length of her back. As they gently stroked her together, Phil said, "Now, Immy, what have you got to say to BJ?"

Imogen was now confidently leading the stroking of BJ as she said, "I'm sorry BJ, I didn't mean to scare you."

Instead of ignoring the issue and pacifying the child - and thereby possibly creating a lifelong phobia, Phil had set about correcting the misunderstanding which had occurred between the dog and child. In consistently dealing with issues in this manner, he taught her to grow up to be an extremely confident and independent young woman.

After experiencing the complete opposite with my own father, I was completely enamored by Phil's obvious parenting skills. It was this trait in him I so admired, that added to my overall attraction to him. With his good head for business and always going after what he wanted as well as his take-charge attitude toward life, it was unusually comforting and reassuring being with him after the haphazard type of existence I had experienced with Russell.

However, there's a reason why experts advise not to get into a relationship or start a new business venture until at least six months to two years after a bereavement. Unfortunately, I did both. Having not dealt with my unresolved issues and emotions I also quickly became overwhelmed with the intricacies involved in starting a business and this led to my overdependence on Phil.

What started as something wonderful became his own personal nightmare. I wasn't fulfilling myself as a person, I was burying myself in my new business venture in an attempt to push past my confused emotions. Then from a state of feeling totally overwhelmed (mostly because I had no idea what I was doing and/or how to market my idea) I would constantly seek his company for his knowledge, or his emotional guidance and support. Just being in his calm presence seemed to make me feel better.

If you don't know how to deal with your own emotions, then you become needy of someone else to fulfil you.

I quickly became needy of Phil. Whereas previously his eyes would light up when he saw me, he started doing a disappearing act and when I did see him I would feel a wall of resistance and frustration emanating from him. I was completely invading his time and his space with a complete disregard for his own need for personal time. It came to the point where he started avoiding me altogether.

At the time, I was devastated because there was nothing I wanted more than to love and to be loved. In my obsessive need, I kept pushing for his attention. This eventually resulted in him accusing me of stalking him and insisting that I leave him alone. I was horrified, yet it would be many years and other failed relationships before I learned and fully understood the vital knowledge and importance of emotional and sexual attraction and how it actually works.

Regardless of all the counselling, time just wasn't healing me. It seemed that my life had become an empty void, stretching infinitely out in front of me. I needed *answers* to make me want to live.

I would often feel sorry for myself thinking how unfair life was and cry myself to sleep.

Even after 12 sessions of psychotherapy I was still feeling emotionally overpowered. Still feeling lost and needy. Flitting from one person to another, asking for advice, trying to find direction. Never trusting my own insights, never feeling completely clear, nor calm or connected. Still a victim of my own perceived weakness, I rarely took responsibility for my thoughts and actions. I continued to rely on others to make me feel better and I frequently relied on others to "rescue me."

My friend Barbara would say to me, "How can you feel lonely when you like being the person you're alone with?" I envied her confidence and her sense of calm, personal empowerment. I wished that I could relate to what she was saying but it would take a long time before I got to that place myself.

I didn't understand that until I succeeded in dealing with emotion I would continue to feel overwhelmed. I thought I wanted answers but my fear of being emotionally overwhelmed in life was paralyzing me. It took a long time to realize that I was simply lacking in skills. Social skills. Communication skills. Sexual skills. Attraction skills. Basic life skills which we all need to be able to function fully and feel fulfilled as human beings.

I needed a skill set of how to survive and flourish as a human. It took me some time to find it.

Even though I had been a consultant in the health and wellness industry for many years, I often felt like I was on an emotional rollercoaster. Still battling depression, anxiety, emotional overwhelm and grief from my losses, I went on a quest to create lasting emotional balance once and for all. Surely there must be a way to overcome all that hypersensitivity?

A friend whom I rarely saw suggested I should give myself time to grieve. So, every day for a year or so, I set aside time each day to grieve. First, I grieved for Russell and then later, Phil. I depressed myself with all my imagined conversations, as well as my self-judgments and recriminations about obsessing over and then losing Phil.

I would feel the tears come and many nights I'd cry myself to sleep. If the tears stopped, I would use memories to manufacture more tears until I felt totally spent. It wasn't helping (and if anything, made me feel worse) but I continued to "give myself time to grieve" religiously. Thinking it would eventually make me feel better but never finding lasting relief. Did it ever make me feel better? No. It just kept me cycling through an unending stream of negative, resistant thoughts and intense emotional responses. I didn't realize that I was self-manufacturing my own mental nightmare and emotional chaos!

The business I had tried so desperately to create had fallen flat. Trying to fill the gap that Russell and then Phil had left in my life I had bulldozed full steam ahead, firmly ignoring well-intended advice from family and friends to first save money for the venture instead of borrowing it. Now I was facing a mountain of debt due to financing a large amount of product on my credit card.

A week before the anniversary of Russell's death, the resulting tension and stress from my failed business attempt combined with my ailing dog BJ and the actual anniversary of Russell dying came to an unexpected head. For the past two years I had been working part time at a rest home hospital as an activities coordinator. I took the elderly residents out on morning trips several times a week in the rest home van which seated twelve including me.

On this fateful morning one of my "regulars" was sitting in one of the seats at the rear near the window. After emptying the van of all other residents, I eased my way toward the back of the van to guide him out. Having been highly independent and gruff in manner in his younger days, he still retained a degree of stubborn independence, always reluctant to receive well-meaning guidance of any sort.

He was also quite deaf. Ignoring (or not hearing) my recommendation to hold the headrest in front of him then pull himself upright and shuffle his way sideways toward the passageway, he reached down and put his knuckles on his seat to push himself up while he levered himself sideways. Wobbly at the best of times, I could see this maneuver was putting his balance off kilter.

Just as I had that thought he lost his balance and started falling in between the rows of seats. Not in the ideal position to rescue him, I reached over the seat in front of me and managed to grab a significant bunch of material around his shirt collar. It wasn't enough to prevent him from going down, but I managed to take most of his weight and prevented him from injury. Unfortunately for me, the twisting motion of him going down wrenched somewhere between my neck and shoulder. I felt a shooting pain race down the length of my arm into my fingers.

Gritting my teeth at the pain, I yelled out for help and one of the duty nurses came running out of the rest home. With the help of another caregiver we bundled the resident out of the van. While one nurse checked him for injuries another asked if I was ok. I was experiencing odd shooting pains emanating randomly from near my shoulder, elbow, little finger and thumb. Along with this I felt shaken and sore but figured it was all only temporary.

However, as the day progressed the pains became more intense and constant. Unable to be of use without my arm, my boss sent me home early. Being a Friday night, I couldn't resist going to the RSA to try and play a few games of snooker. But I couldn't keep my mind on the game because of the shooting pains in my arm and hand. And as the evening progressed it became impossible to make a bridge with my left hand to accurately position the cue. Disappointed in my inability to play, I resigned myself to going home early from there too.

I hardly had any sleep that night and by the next morning I was in agony. Every time I marginally moved my thumb I would shriek in pain. It hurt when I moved, and it hurt when I didn't move. The most basic of activities I couldn't perform without experiencing that excruciating pain.

Whereas in the past acupuncture had healed every malady for me, with this injury it did absolutely nothing to ease the pain. Two weeks later I was still off work with no improvement in sight.

What made everything worse was that my white dog BJ was ailing and appearing to be near her end. Being 14, she had been a huge part of my life, my next best friend after Russell. BJ had always acted like a young, active, vibrant dog but she aged overnight when Russell passed.

Russell had been her best friend and like me she was totally devastated when he died.

I watched BJ rapidly deteriorate in the first year of Russell's passing but I totally resisted those thoughts. I had wanted for her to pass quickly like Russell did, but it just didn't happen that way. BJ had given up on life and was waiting to die and there was nothing I could do about it.

Two weeks after my accident she would lie up in the back garden where tomatoes were growing wild, making sad noises and looking absolutely miserable. It broke my heart. I was barely coping with the pain in my arm and the anniversary of Russell passing and now I could sense that I was losing her too.

Even when it began raining, she wouldn't move. I took a blanket up to where she was lying and made us a lean-to to keep the rain off her. She absolutely refused to come inside, and I was too afraid to leave her by herself. I was terrified that she would die without me being there. I couldn't let that happen.

I resisted the fact that she was dying. I couldn't bear the thought of being abandoned by my second-best friend – and the huge feeling of loneliness which seemed to go with the thought of it.

Because I was resisting how she was dying, I tried to control it. I finally managed to coax her inside for the night. Her kidneys had given out on her and she yelped in pain every time she moved. It was a long night for both of us. She seemed even more miserable being inside than out so the next morning I helped her limp and yelp her way outside to the back yard to lie woefully in the sun.

BJ had touched the lives of many right from when she was a small, squirming flea ridden puppy rescued from a family who couldn't afford to keep the puppies of their own beloved dog. Letting go of her was almost harder than letting go of Russell. Probably because I watched death slowly take BJ. She started dying when Russell left us.

By this time, I couldn't control my emotion, tears were pouring down my face. I knew she was in agony and I couldn't handle her pain any longer. I felt guilty and angry. I cursed and swore at Russell, I had been informed by a clairvoyant friend that he would come and get BJ when it was time for her to pass. Angry, upset, disappointed and feeling total despair that I wasn't sensing any sign of his spirit, in desperation I drove BJ to the vet.

The vet said that her kidneys had failed, and it was just a matter of time before she died. He told me that it would be a slow and horrible death. I decided the more loving option would be to give her the injection. But I told the vet that we had to wait because Russell aka BJ's dad had promised to be there (Russell and I never had children, our dogs had always been our kids) and I needed to give him another five minutes.

I'm not a religious person, yet I have a strong belief that we are more than just a physical body and that we become more complete within ourselves when we die. However, when I told the vet that her "dad" was in spirit form, his eyebrows shot to the ceiling before he hastily turned away and started busying himself with preparing her injection!

I was feeling a huge amount of anguish over her condition, but BJ was just looking at me trustingly as though she was waiting, too. I closed my eyes, felt the warmth of her fur, felt into the discomfort of my own resistance and had the following vision:

BJ was walking with me in a beautiful meadow filled with tall, vibrant flowers. As I watched, I saw Russell walking towards us. For a brief moment, I opened my eyes and told the vet that her father was here now, that he could continue with the injection. I saw the vet's eyebrows shoot to the ceiling once more before I closed my eyes. I went back into the feeling and allowed the vision to continue.

Just as I closed my eyes, the vision started again, BJ saw Russell. Her ears perked up – she was SO excited. She bounded over to him and pulled up abruptly; then alternated between licking him and barking at him excitedly. She was ecstatic! As I watched, Russell wrapped his arms around her, gave her a big hug and looking up he smiled at me briefly before turning away. Just as they turned and started walking away together, I heard the vet say: "Oh my God, she died... just before I injected her..."

Life doesn't always happen as we plan it, but sometimes magic happens anyway.

My Search for Answers

Unfortunately, after BJ died I was back on my rollercoaster ride of resistance toward my emotional and physical pain. Physiotherapy had followed the failed attempt at healing via acupuncture. Twelve more treatments of physio and still no improvement in my condition. Four months later my doctor referred me to a neurologist who asked me a whole bunch of questions and then determined that as well as having quite severe nerve damage I was also clinically depressed. He prescribed Amitriptyline to help me cope with the pain and to "take the edge" off my emotions.

I remained a victim of my own thoughts for about another six months before I decided that it was time to take charge of my life. Although still in pain, I ditched the medication. I practiced relaxation techniques. I researched nutritional supplements to support my well-being. They didn't completely remove the pain, but they did far more to empower me as a person than the drugs ever did.

Another six months passed and my arm (for the most part) was healed, even though I had been told by the medical specialists that I would probably never regain full use of it. There's always something so delicious about proving the medical specialists to be wrong! I would go on to surprise the medical profession in many other ways too!

While I was in the welfare system I made the most of the free business training courses they made available and focused my attention on achieving a full recovery. I have always been fiercely proud as a person and this was a most humbling period of my life. It had been a difficult time financially as my credit card's minimum payment each month was well over half of what I was receiving on the benefit. It was only Pat's support in keeping my boarding fee low which enabled me to avoid financial bankruptcy. The next part of my story started to provide the answers I had so desperately been seeking.

The various therapies including psychotherapy and counselling helped me to understand myself as a person, but I wasn't given the *answers* of how to take charge and be in control of my own emotional and sexual fulfilment. It didn't teach me how to achieve orgasm - and that's what I really wanted, I wanted to be in charge of my own body!

Because I was unable to find lasting answers I pledged to dedicate the rest of my life to figuring them out. I had no desire to stay stuck in repeating my story and so left no stone unturned in my quest. I also made it my mission to solve male and female sex problems. There was *no way* I wanted to enter another relationship also without knowing how to sexually fulfil myself and a partner. I spent the next several years researching and developing methods.

It was about this time that I was introduced to tantric healing principles. As well as teaching Tantra, Natalie and her husband (at the time) had also developed a different technique for dealing with emotions. I had attended one of their evening talks on emotion and healing and after experiencing some relief, decided to give their workshop a go.

After denying myself my emotions for so many years, initially it felt liberating to experience the sounds related to them. I would eagerly allow the tears and wailing and other loud sounds which emanated from me, to "release" my old, pent-up emotions. While it was better than my previous suppression of emotions, after a while it felt over-the-top unnecessary. And it proved to be disconcerting for anyone within hearing distance who had no idea what was going on!

Tantra was a little more helpful on the sexual side of things in that I experienced my first orgasm. I then spent several years learning, researching and developing Tantric methods to solve sex problems. I eventually concluded that Tantric techniques were complicated and confusing. Results were random and inconsistent and therefore didn't provide a complete answer for solving either gender's sexual dysfunction problems.

Eventually I devised an effective method for overcoming anxiety and emotional overwhelm. One of my clients likened my emotional healing technique to being similar to Eckhart Tolle but easier to understand. From working with Natalie, I had determined that emotions don't manifest outside of your body. Building on this concept, I then figured that emotions only appear to increase when you're resistant to experiencing them. I term this as being in a state of emotional resistance and this is the reason you will feel further disconnected from yourself.

The truth is that you can't separate yourself from your emotions without causing an unresolved division within yourself. Also, you can't resist experiencing your emotions without your mind becoming involved in the conflict. Every time you resist your emotions, you resist feeling connected and at ease, within yourself and with everyone else.

The unique technique I personally figured out, enables any person to neutralize strong or overwhelming emotions within seconds. This results in feeling clear, calm and connected with yourself and others. If you've listened to any of the Abraham-Hicks recordings, you'll recognize this feeling as being "in the Vortex". My technique is one of the fastest and easiest ways to immediately put yourself into that state of zero-resistance and to switch back into it whenever you notice the mental, emotional or physical discomfort associated with switching out!

I was later hooked up to a Heart Math machine which registers your state in between heart beats. I registered 100% coherence state (anything over 65% is unheard of) for over two minutes while I applied my unique technique. It's a highly effective way to feel relaxed, calm and connected.

Within a short period of time, people were being referred to me. Men, women and teens suffering from depression, anxiety, feeling disconnected from themselves and from others. I saw people from all walks of life. It didn't seem to matter if they were rich or poor, beautiful to look at or plain, everyone was suffering from these problems! Ultimately, I defined this condition as "Humanitis." Simply put, the condition of being human. Emotional overwhelm is a common plight which seems to have the same effect on everyone.

Most of us get caught up in the thoughts of why we think we're feeling any particular way. This consistently constant negative mental chatter is what can lead us down the thinking slide toward suicide.

One day I received a distressed call from a young 20-year-old man on the brink of suicide. Completely overwhelmed with the direction his life was taking, he couldn't see a way out of his problems. He was constantly cycling between anxiety and fear, then anxiety and despair. His constant mental chatter was driving him crazy and he feared for his sanity.

During his session with me, I explained how it's common to get caught up in our thoughts about why we think we're feeling a certain way... how it's this very thing which causes resistance and other emotional responses which we try to stop because we want to feel better... and how *this* prevents us from feeling peaceful, calm and connected with ourselves and others. I then taught him my technique for neutralizing unwanted emotions.

As we talked, and he explained more of his situation, I could see by his expression whenever an emotional response was triggered. Each time this happened, I would interrupt his dialogue and guide him to switch his attention to allow the physical discomfort of the emotional response so that in that moment, he could feel better.

I knew from experience that simply talking about his issues wouldn't get him to where he wanted to be and would keep him stuck. It really doesn't matter what stories we have about why we're feeling miserable. Mentally, physically and emotionally, *we cannot feel better* until we stop being emotionally resistant and allow each emotional response to pass.

I knew he needed to restore his sense of belief in himself, so I pointed him in the right direction by getting him in the habit of interrupting his own dialogue each time an emotional response was triggered. By recognizing an emotional response, he could then turn his emotion around, so he didn't mentally entangle himself. This enabled him to know for sure that he *did* have total control over his emotions as well as the effect emotions would always have on him.

Within less than an hour into our session, he was grinning ear-to-ear and telling me that he was now excited about his future... that he felt he now had the skills to not only cope with life's challenges but to actually *enjoy* his life.

As he was leaving he said that I had been his last hope and admitted that prior to our session he had been on his way to commit suicide. On parting, he said, "But I don't want (or need) to do that anymore, now I've got *answers* and I know for sure that I can change how my emotions affect me... and I know how I can keep feeling better!"

All he had needed was to understand how to master his emotions, so he could navigate through life's challenges with more ease.

We can't change the way our brain responds to certain thoughts, memories and situations with an emotional response. But we can change the way each emotional response plays out.

In the process of developing my method I became involved in various personal development groups, ran emotional empowerment groups and workshops and became a sought-after speaker to share my unique knowledge and insights at events. Finally, my life had purpose!

In the past, I had been known by my family members to be short-sighted at times for my failure to recognize the needs of others. It wasn't that I didn't care, it's more that I just didn't notice.

There are many humble people on this planet who are so busy helping others that they ask nothing for themselves. My mother is one of these people and so was Russell's mother.

For many years I ignored some of Pat's obvious needs. I told myself at the time that if she wanted something from me, she should ask me or tell me herself. But she never did. Therefore, I never made the concessions which would have made her life easier. Russell's sister has severe Asperger's and Pat spent countless hours repeatedly consoling her incessant demands. It was exhausting just listening to them. Having to constantly deal with his sister's frequent, unwanted visits and her loud, argumentative attitude for all those years added to my growing resistance toward Russell's family members.

After Russell died, Pat invited me to continue living there with her. Several years later she fell and badly broke her hip. While in hospital she suffered a stroke. Then another. The family had to subdivide the property to pay for her ongoing care in an aged-care hospital facility. My personal development business had been picking up for a while, I was easily able to afford the market rent they were now asking me to pay.

It was during these turbulent years that I had an epiphany. This happened one day when Russell's sister in law came to do some work on the property. I don't remember how it started, but she totally blew a fuse. I had only recently figured out my technique for dealing with strong emotions and boy, did I get a chance to practice it on this day!

For many years she had observed the uncaring and selfish manner with which Russell and I had treated his mother, without his sister in law ever having said a word. Over the years she had harbored many judgmental thoughts but never expressed them out loud.

Everything that she had ever thought about saying to me began pouring out of her mouth. Until I heard her I hadn't realized the extent of my selfishness. Looking back, it was possibly born from my years of trying to survive as well as not knowing how to effectively communicate with others. I definitely lacked in social skills in the earlier portion of my life!

When she was finally spent, she looked at me searchingly, "I don't understand why you did this, how could you have been like that, so selfish?"

With those words, another intense emotional response in me was triggered. It felt intense and uncomfortable, I looked her in the eye as I allowed the brief physically uncomfortable moment to pass. Then, feeling totally calm, I looked at her and said, "Because I didn't know what I know now. I'm so sorry for all the pain I've caused you and your family."

The simple truth acknowledged her as a person and eased her pain. It also allowed her to express emotions which had been suppressed for many years. The issue had contaminated her thought pattern, cycling around inside her head awaiting a chance for release. Eventually after this salvo, I believe she experienced a feeling of satisfaction and peace. This is the end result we are all trying to realize when we have emotional resistance.

That day was such a wake-up call! What a gift she gave me that day! Speaking your truth is one of the most powerful gifts you can give another person. It most certainly has been for me.

My point is that you can't ever change what is perceived to be a problem if you don't understand it in the first place. Most people are too polite to comment. When someone has a behavioral pattern, which is obviously damaging to themselves and others, most people won't interfere or become involved. Many will analyze the situation for days on end without ever saying a word to the person involved. This means that the affected person never rectifies the controversy they could quite easily change with the right knowledge.

Having produced an effective answer for solving anxiety and achieving emotional stability, I was still on my quest to provide answers to solve male and female sex problems.

The most unexpected answer was to come to me. Russell's sister in law informed me that I was living at the house on borrowed time. His sister with Asperger's was insisting that she move back into the family home. Because of her demanding behavior which alienated all attempts at finding her alternative accommodation, there seemed no other answer. After living in their family home for nearly 16 years, I was given my final notice.

There was a part of me which had wanted to move for such a long time. Having grown within myself and really starting to like myself as a person, I felt ready for the change.

With just two weeks remaining on my lease I decided that it would be ok to share a house. I had barely posted an ad online when I received a phone call. The caller, Paul and I hit it off right away. He asked what I did for hobbies and when I mentioned I loved playing pool, he said he used to play snooker for money. We talked for over an hour on that first call, sharing our stories and life experiences.

He said he had found an awesome house in the city which had recently been fully refurbished and needed a flat mate to share the expenses. Paul completely wooed me. After explaining my work, he said I could have two of the three rooms and just pay half the rent. It seemed too good a deal to pass.

He then warned me of the fact that he was always right. With a carefree laugh in my voice I replied that it would be interesting because I was always right too! Little did I know that comment would come back to bite me. I was about to start my greatest education of all!

Although intending to move in as house-mates we quickly became more than that. I had been in a few short-term relationships since Phil, none of which worked out for me. The most recent had been someone who just didn't fire up the passion which Phil had unleashed in me. I didn't want to hurt him so instead of telling him he wasn't right for me in a relationship, I just kind of backed off until he ended the relationship in frustration.

It's important to speak the truth of a matter as any-thing less than that will still result in pain for the other person involved, sometimes even more so. We all know how it feels when we know something is wrong or off, but nothing is being communicated to us. The reality is when something's not being communicated the other person feels the rejection of not being told the truth.

At this point in my life I had also been going through a weird kind of health issue. Perhaps it was the culmination of stress caused by my resistant thoughts and emotions over the years. I had the most awful stomach cramps for several months, but I also had an aversion to doctors and taking medications. Which is why I decided not to go to the doctor. I just figured that eventually the pains would go away, and my body would heal by itself.

It was literally just a few weeks after the end of the previous relationship when I met Paul. Where I had felt little sexual attraction for the last guy, with this one the attraction was through the roof! I was back to one of my old behaviors, having early sex in the hope of creating a meaningful relationship.

Paul was different to any man I had previously met. His knowledge on every subject vast, he was the absolute best at everything. When he was at school they wanted to advance him *four* years ahead academically! He excelled in art. One day he had shown his pointillism drawing to Rei Hamon, a world-renowned pointillism artist. Initially agreeing to giving him just 10 minutes of his time, Rei sat staring at Paul's drawing with an awestruck expression on his face for over an hour, questioning how Paul could possibly have made the rocks and the bush look so real.

He excelled in sports. When in high school he played for the local adult cricket team as well as qualifying to play in the rugby team although his parents wouldn't allow it. He excelled in dance and he excelled in music. Everything he put his mind to, he excelled at. The man is a natural. As well as inadvertently falling into a relationship with me he also became my greatest mentor.

Paul had come from a long line of Tohunga (indigenous teachers/mentors.) Any challenge which I encountered he would examine it from all angles and suggest a course of logical action. When I frequently mentioned I had sore shoulders, he determined I was repetitively using some arm and shoulder muscles without utilizing others which was causing weaknesses and muscle imbalances. He pulled out a set of weights and gave me four exercises to perform daily. As well as reducing the tension in my shoulders this unexpectedly solved another issue! Having been mortified as a teen when my breasts stopped growing beyond what could only be described as "pods," after about six months Paul's exercises increased my bra cup by two full sizes!

His knowledge on imbalances and alignment were self-learned. About 30 years prior he had been super fit, strong, and cycling 80 km most days. One night while out cycling he was hit by a drunk driver and smashed 50 feet down the road. It was a hit and run, the driver had left him for dead. The taxi driver who found him lying in a pool of blood thought that he *was* dead. Rushed to hospital, Paul lay in a coma clinging to life. He had landed on his head (no cycle helmets in those days) the handlebars of the bike had damaged the nerves in his chest, his lower back was cracked, and his foot injured. His right ear had fused shut with the force of the impact and the surgeon had to cut that area open and form a new ear opening. It was two days before he regained consciousness.

Paul is one tough cookie. Appearing to mostly recover after a period of several months, a couple of years later his back started to rapidly deteriorate. He then literally became a cripple overnight. For three years he could barely take a few steps without falling down in an agonizing heap, then being unable to move for several hours due to the unbearable pain.

He was then told he might never walk again and was eventually given the option of a new surgery. Trusting in his own ability to analyze the situation and apply a logical solution he refused the surgery and after a couple of years of self-manipulation he asked the surgeon to instead put him in traction. He had a theory and wanted to test it. Paul had developed a unique technique over the years and he believed it would help his body heal. It all started with being in correct alignment, hence the requirement for traction.

The doctors told him to never do any heavy lifting, so he then got himself a job at an engineering shop and started heavy lifting. He figured the best thing he could do for himself was to become strong again. Although initially it was agony, he persevered knowing that he needed to strengthen his body to be able to make a full recovery.

For the most part, he healed himself. Other than the pain he still experienced in his left foot. Several years later when he was out hiking with a friend he noticed he was placing this foot pointing directly ahead instead of turning it out slightly like his other foot was naturally placed.

Logically contemplating the ramifications of this discovery, he purposely turned his left foot slightly outward like the other foot (think five to one on a clock face) and practiced walking this way. He experienced slight relief, so he made a few more modifications to his gait and continued with this practice. After a few months, the pain completely left his ankle and moved into his knee. Then it moved out of his knee and into his hip. Then out of his hip and into his lower back. Then up to his upper back, then a few months later the pain was completely gone. To this day, his doctor still describes him as a walking miracle. He recently turned 67 and most people think he's under fifty.

Paul teaches alignment. He discovered after his long absence from playing snooker due to his injury that he could no longer pot balls with the accuracy he had previously possessed. In his days of hustling snooker for money he had beaten several world class players. While playing for money he had made a 78-point break playing with just one arm. As was his way, Paul applied logic and came to the conclusion that the extreme exercising he had undertaken to build up his muscle strength had totally changed his physique. By now he was moving up to two tons of steel a day at work.

With this understanding, he devised a new 12-point procedure for approaching the balls on the snooker table. Using this alignment strategy, he was able to restore his previous ability within a few short weeks. Regardless of taking any time off playing in the future he could reapply this procedure at any time to fast pace his return to his playing level. Although he recovered from the accident he was never the same standard of player he was prior to being hit by the car.

Paul can confidently take any person who plays any sport, and take their game through the stratosphere with this unique technique. And it doesn't just apply to sport, it applies to everything in life. As I was about to find out.

After observing clients coming and going from the house, Paul would ask me about my work and how I went about it. When I explained about tantra and how it works he said, "I bet most of your clients don't get results from that method. Let me tell you why..." He then explained how I was confusing their brain with those tantric techniques.

Of course, I hotly debated this fact as my customer's feedback was showing reasonable results. Then he looked at me searchingly and said, "How about I teach you a method which will give your clients the results they're *really* hoping for?"

He continued to question my methods to solve these problems and passed unique knowledge to me over time. He explained how we can influence our brain with specific thoughts as well as aligning our physical actions. He called this the Switching Technique. Interestingly, this switching technique fully explained my unique method for overcoming emotional challenges. I'll explain this method in detail later in this book, so you can apply it in your life too.

At first his knowledge was overpowering. I was resistant to adapt it to my knowledge base for solving sex problems because it brought into question everything I had learned up to that point.

Then one day I tried his teaching on a client who mentioned he had a premature ejaculation problem. I was stunned with the result the client reported and sent a text message to Paul saying he "got it in an hour and a half!" Incredible! Not weeks or months, no medication, just an explanation and the problem solved. Paul just replied, "I told you it would work!"

The next client reported premature ejaculation AND erectile dysfunction. I explained the Switching Technique. ONE week later, this 72-year-old phoned to tell me both of those problems were now solved!

I then applied the same fundamentals to myself to try and rid myself of the "monkey on *my* back!"

This knowledge immediately solved my problem of being unable to consistently achieve orgasm. There was just no comparison to other techniques I had tried. By using the Switching Technique, I was now able to orgasm "on demand" during masturbation, foreplay *and* intercourse! *Every time* I engaged in sexual activity I had success and I could now switch my libido on and off with ease.

Later, when I reached my mid-forties and started experiencing inner vaginal dryness, I developed a "Switch" which immediately solves that problem too.

All these successes, just by correctly switching my focus? I had finally found the missing link to solving sex problems!

After suffering through that year of sexual abuse and thinking my internal wiring was all screwed, my body was now responding normally! It seemed ridiculously easy to gain emotional and sexual fulfilment. Suddenly life became a much more enjoyable game to play. After all those years of suffering mentally and emotionally due to assuming I was sexually deficient, I was experiencing the stellar opposite.

Sexual intimacy became fun and exciting. I further researched how the brain works, and completed a diploma in Cognitive Behavioral Therapy and also became certified in nutrition.

Just when the sex was getting good... the intensity of the stomach cramps I experienced was worsening. Although I had a super clean diet (and avoided wheat, dairy, sugar, trans fats and preservatives) it felt like I was being repeatedly stabbed randomly throughout my gastrointestinal tract. The cramps were debilitating. For several months, I endured the pain with my teeth firmly grit together. Many times, I would curl up in bed crying with the pain and frustration of it. Paul insisted I get medical attention. We needed to know one way or the other, what was causing the pain.

Because if you don't know what the problem is, you can't plan a solid strategy to solve it.

One of Paul's most frequent sayings is that the conscious mind lies, cheats and makes excuses. He convinced me to deal with the gut pain problem by going to the doctor... which led to going to the hospital for tests. A few months later a specialist reported that I had ulcerative colitis. He also said I appeared to be doing a pretty good job of healing myself.

At the time of that health issue when I was experiencing a great deal of pain, I wasn't taking any time to fulfil myself as a person with activities I enjoyed. I completely relied on Paul to entertain me and barely left the house.

Because of the pain I was in, I was trying to ignore the physical discomfort in my body. This meant that when the related emotional responses were triggered, I was ignoring them too.

In the weekend, I wanted to go everywhere with Paul. Even if he just wanted to pop down to the hardware shop, I wanted to go for a ride. I could sense that this was annoying for him, however, I decided that my need for comfort was greater and was relying on his company to make me feel better. Kind of like when I was with Phil.

From his perspective, he wasn't getting any time to himself, I was smothering him with my neediness. Although it seemed like an innocent plea for support, I was being irresponsible by not meeting any of my own emotional needs. Eventually, the ongoing pressure resulting from my neediness and Paul's resistance to it, built-up and damaged our relationship.

I was yet to understand how attraction works.

Although he was painfully brutal with his observations of people, I was fascinated with Paul's ability to apply logic and reason. Even when I thought I had good reason to be upset, he would supply another logical point of view which I never would have become aware of myself. Regardless of our different wants and needs, the learning aspect was addictive.

But his blatantly honest verbal brutality made him difficult to live with and be in a relationship with.

I had never met anyone who would correct my grammar as precisely as Paul. Although my Mum came close. I was most certainly making up for the lack of attention to detail I produced at high school as Paul would pounce on every misuse of a word!

He also triggered me like no one else could. We would argue and debate and fight and then make up and ten days later start the whole process again. It was exhausting but I was addicted to his knowledge and I was addicted to the feeling of how great our relationship was when we weren't fighting. We eventually decided that we weren't compatible as a couple. However, since we got on well sharing the house together we decided to move into our separate rooms and go back to the original plan of being "housemates." He continued to mentor me and increase my knowledge base on many subjects.

He remains my trusted friend, mentor and advisor and helped me develop a revolutionary system for solving male and female sex problems. Common sex problems including performance anxiety, premature ejaculation, erectile dysfunction, low libido and being unable to achieve orgasm can now be easily solved (more on that in Part 2.)

Together we developed the concept of "The A Game" and how vital it is to not disregard your partner's needs. Remember that if your partner mentions something once, they have probably thought deeply on it many times. If you have a problem, deal with the problem and you no longer have a problem. Because if you ignore the problem it will become bigger and cause more problems!

For any relationship to thrive as well as contributing to the mutual benefit of both partners, you must also take steps to fulfil yourself as a person. Your partner isn't responsible for doing this for you.

Instead of relying on your partner to make you feel good about yourself, be responsible for this undertaking yourself. Allow all emotional responses to resolve when they're triggered. Stop allowing your mind to make excuses. Your partner is not responsible for fulfilling you as a person, you are.

I've always believed that there's an answer to every problem and if we firmly believe we will find the answer, we will eventually be led to it. One day I was at the local village on my way to buy some meat from the organic butcher. I passed a sign on a sandwich board which said something like: "We improve your smile." Curious as to what they could do for me, I followed the arrow down to a dental clinic and made my way inside. After carefully investigating the mess in which my teeth had been rearranged by the orthodontist many years prior, the dentist set upon planning a dental artistry strategy to make my smile more acceptable to me.

She filed my big artificial tooth down to a more natural size and built the smaller tooth up to match it. No more having to rearrange my tongue to try and hide my mismatched teeth, it felt so delicious to just relax and smile.

One by one, I was resolving the issues that had plagued my confidence and self-esteem. I was also developing my techniques to help others. Yet I was still missing an essential link. Attraction. It was the one thing separating me from having the complete answer... and separating me from a potential mate.

Without understanding how attraction works, we unwittingly drive others away from us.

The Final Piece of the Puzzle

I learned the hard way about attraction. This next life lesson started at my friend Angela's birthday party. A group of us met at a Japanese restaurant where we were to celebrate her birthday. Standing in the foyer waiting for all her guests to arrive, I was surreptitiously watching one of her friends. I hadn't met him before. He had an engaging, mischievous look about him which I found endearing.

Because there were so many of us we couldn't all fit around one seating area. When one of Angela's friends arrived late, we all shuffled one over and I ended up being seated next to the mystery man. We joked and chatted and relaxed and had fun and he totally charmed me.

I mentioned to my friend the next day that I liked him and suggested she give him my number.

Males like to compete for a woman's attention. So, when all is given on a platter, or a woman tries to prove how amazing she is with her nurturing skills, it causes many a man to lose attention and run for the hills.

Way back when Phil had met me, I had appeared independent in my relationship with Russell. Often when we visited the twins' house, I would read or otherwise entertain myself while they drank. I didn't appear needy, so it was a great shock to him when that's exactly how I acted with him.

With Paul, my neediness had developed due to the emotional responses I repressed which were mostly associated with my illness.

The new mystery man Steve had a mysterious health issue which I took upon myself to solve. Instead of allowing him to be the strong man he is, I inundated him with possible "solutions" to cure him of his malady.

Whereas initially when we had started dating he called me "Mischief," within a month he was backing away from my advances and had renamed me "Fluffy". I was horrified but couldn't seem to stop myself from fussing. Via his constant withdrawals to my advances we parted ways. I then decided that enough was enough. There was an obvious gap in my knowledge base and it was time to get an education on how attraction really works. However, I was also to learn about the importance of paying attention!

2014 went off with a bang for me... literally. I was out on a yacht with Angela and a couple of friends. Moored near an island in the harbor and sitting in the cockpit relaxing, Steve (now no more than my friend) set to the task of catching breakfast.

The fish were biting that morning and he called out excitedly that he had just caught another one. I jumped out of the cockpit to have a look, then stepped back down into the cockpit contemplating launching myself diagonally back into my seat on the other side.

In the moment I was about to launch, another friend asked me a question. Instead of stopping and pausing to answer his question, I turned my head to look at him and continued launching myself back into my seat. Unfortunately, by turning my head away from my task I had adversely affected my co-ordination.

Instead of arriving safely back in my seat, I launched myself directly into the yacht boom over-head. With a resounding "THUNK!!" my head impacted the steel boom. Oh, the pain! My eyes closed with the intensity of the pain, I gingerly reached out to feel for the seat, so I could carefully sit down. It felt like a dozen skyrockets were being launched inside my head.

The pain was horrendous. I sat as still as I could and it was a couple of minutes before I could speak. Although I tried to make light of it, it hurt for my eyes to be open and felt like my head had been split with an axe. In an instant, I went from being relaxed and happy, to feeling nauseated, off balance and miserable. It took over 12 months to completely heal this injury.

When you're sick or injured it's important to not allow your mind to lie, cheat and make excuses. Because it will. It will naturally compare what you don't have to what you did have. Then it will compare what you had, to what you might not have in future. Our mind is in constant analysis.

I know how challenging it can be to feel sick, tired and sore for a long period of time. Remember to allow all emotional responses to pass so you can relax and be less reliant on other people to make you feel fulfilled as a human being.

Another cool thing you can do when in recovery mode is to *remember* how good it feels when you indulge in the activities which fulfil you as a person. As you remember these things, you connect with the feel-good feelings you have associated with these activities. It's part of The Switching Technique. This helps to regulate your breathing, heart rate, blood pressure and relax your muscles... and is what makes you feel better.

In the past when you have been ill or recovering from an injury you may have judged the fact that you could not actively participate in those tasks! Judgements such as those will always trigger an emotional response and if you try to block THAT then you prevent yourself from feeling better.

In the time between Steve ending what had barely started between us and my unfortunate demise with the yacht boom, I had dedicated several months and resources to learning about attraction and how it works. It all made complete sense and looking back over my life experience I could see what caused the initial attraction between me and my various partners to go completely out of alignment.

It also became obvious to me that to be attractive to someone else, you need to maintain emotional alignment within yourself. Because resistant emotions affect attraction and libido!

Armed with my already in-depth understanding relating to resistance, emotions, sex and libido, I now had the final piece of the puzzle.

Important Note for Readers

It's important to note the insights featured in this book are the end result of my own research and discovery. They are not presented with any medical or psychological case studies. I do not claim any warranty for what is written which would bear any similarity to the medical profession.

I have been audited for authenticity by my government and testimony was given by a medical specialist who underwent a remedial session with me. He stated that he is familiar with my methodology and recommends my treatment method.

The descriptions offered in this book are for the purposes of easy understanding of the subject matter in layman's terms and not meant to displace any theories offered by philosophers, psychologists and scientists.

More testimonies from doctors who undertook my programs:

RE: Recommendation to Jacqui Olliver

"I am 2000% happy with your program. I am a medical doctor in the allopathic system of medicine. I have read sexology and all the associated medical literature extensively. I know in medicine there is no treatment more effective than your program. I have tried many types of drugs, consultation with many therapists and many herbs and Ayurveda. Your discovery and solution to sex problem in males is 2000 times better than all other pills and suggestions combined.

This above statement I am giving from my personal experience of following Jacqui Olliver's program for men.

Her treatment and protocol are based on physiology and mechanism of doing sex. Her knowledge and perception about the problem are really amazing. Her theory and protocol are scientific and gives 100% result to me.

I will recommend her treatment to all males even if he may or may not suffer sexual problems because every male now has some sort of sexual problem due to very basic lack of training. Every person has scope for improvement.

Now what we are seeing as medical doctors are men not satisfied with life because they are not satisfied in bed during sex, this is the thing everybody is hiding. I recommend this program for every male to follow. This will definitely make him feel a more confident and well-balanced male, especially during sex.

You have made a wonderful discovery mam. I like to thank you again. Please feel free to ask me how I can help you spread this information for the benefit of humanity. Thanks a lot for your amazing program which has changed my life. I again thank you for serving humanity in such a wonderful way.

You can quote my statements anywhere you want."

Dr Vijay Raghavan, Diabetes and Metabolic Specialist for Incurable Diseases

"I've been to medical conferences all around the world, searching for an answer to my ED problem which started occurring after prostate surgery. No medical specialists are able to provide a permanent solution for erectile dysfunction – they have no idea how to solve it. Jacqui offered a completely different perspective – I am amazed at how well this technique works! Sometimes I lose focus and start losing the erection – but now I know how to immediately get it back!"

Brian, Medical Specialist, Erectile Dysfunction after Prostate Surgery

PART 2

If You Have a Problem, Deal with the Problem and You No Longer Have a Problem

The first half of my book was to describe my life from "WHOA TO GO!" But unfortunately, it never turned out that way. My life was so confused with a lack of social skills and the required knowledge that it actually went from "GO TO WHOA!" There was an underlying lack of empathy from people close to me which made me adopt the same mirror image response to my life. I admit that I never had the foresight to verbally ask for interaction but was that my job to do so? After all, I was only a child. The accrued emotional suppression I suffered from my childhood continued through to my adult years. This perpetual merry-go-round of uncertainty affected me immensely to the point where I suffered from sexual incompetence. This lead to promiscuity as a means of gaining acceptance from my peers, which in hindsight is absolutely wrong.

I wrongly attributed all my problems to being sexually abused as a teen. This included my inability to sexually function properly. This affected me in every relationship I had from my teen years to adulthood. There was no sense of sexual satisfaction to the point that I never orgasmed. This in turn infected the interactions I received from my partners. Eventually, they too became sexually deficient or defective.

All in all, I wrong footed myself all my life until just recently. I was devastated on a personal level. I struggled to function as a normal human being and

I'm not even talking about sexually. As a person, I struggled to slot into anything normal. This was accentuated by my inability to understand the mechanics of being normal, so I developed a tough cookie attitude. If I couldn't be normal I would try to be super normal. To achieve this, I adopted a male psyche in my drive to be competitive. Much later in my life I had an epiphany that I would discover the answer and share it with everyone who suffered like I did. Therefore, I undertook a quest to learn as much as I could about my problem.

Eventually I was lucky enough to meet a person who had figured this out. I initially resisted this knowledge as it challenged every remedy I had learned in the last 20 years. But when I reluctantly tried this technique it solved my client's problem in a couple of hours. Unbelievable! So, I changed tact and learned as much from him as I could. This method suddenly made me understand the problems I had inherited from the earlier part of my life! Now I had the right ammunition!

My vision was to share part of this teaching to solve a problem which plagues millions of people worldwide. Unresolved emotions can devastate both individuals and couples. Sex may be known as the glue which holds a relationship together but resistance and unresolved emotions will just as powerfully tear the relationship apart.

Solving sexual dysfunctions and restoring emotional balance are essential parts of the puzzle. However, attraction embellishes libido as well as emotional connection and therefore provides the primary pillar to ensure a strong foundation for every relationship.

How to Achieve Real EASY Love

Attraction had been one of the main ingredients I didn't understand properly and it prevented me from achieving a balanced two-way loving relationship. I had taken it upon myself to lean on my partner instead of sharing the essence of the relationship. This ultimately had a one-way directional flow which made the relationship lopsided and eventually my partner lost interest in me.

Without a solid foundational understanding of how attraction works, emotional balance cannot be maintained. This is because craving an emotional connection with another person eventually becomes a mental and physical obsession. Yet without each individual attaining a proper emotional balance you cannot function as a complete person. This imbalance causes you to become needy of another person which then negatively affects both people's reasons for attraction. It's a vicious cycle which many people fall victim to.

I primarily focus on solving sexual dysfunction problems and helping clients understand how to feel relaxed, confident and connected in themselves and in their relationships.

The concept for Real EASY Love was initiated when I started decoding all the essential segments of EASY which are:

Emotional balance
Attraction alignment
Sexual function
You and your partner

Whether you're on your own or in a relationship with another person, being emotionally balanced is essential for achieving and sustaining peace of mind and body. In an intimate relationship, there are three essential components:

Sex
Emotional connection
Attraction alignment

Sex... is to TOTALLY understand all components which complement the sexual act.

Emotional connection... is understanding the emotional interaction between two people and how it binds the relationship together.

Attraction alignment... is the initial reason why having that balance both as an individual or couple has integrated the desire to interact together.

This is a good recipe for a "SEA" of love! Get the balance right and it will mostly be smooth sailing.

Get these confused and you will struggle to communicate clearly and constantly feel like you're losing your grip on reality.

This is because:

Resistant
Emotions
Alter
Life!

Resistant emotions also affect attraction and libido. It's only when attaining a higher degree of personal balance that you can:

Leave
Out
Victim
Entanglements!

While some of your life experiences may have made you feel like a victim, you only continue to be a victim when you indulge in the resistant thoughts and emotions which keep you constantly trapped in a victim mode.

Because ignorance without action can't help you, you need to additionally upgrade your knowledge base and then take steps to end the problems you are facing.

I dedicated the stories in part one of this book (my life-generated PhD) to help you understand and relate to the impediments related to resistance, emotions, attraction and libido. To stop feeling overwhelmed and lost you just need to know how to maintain the correct balance. It's impossible to feel fulfilled as a person when resistant emotions are affecting your ability to connect with yourself and to others and make logical decisions.

Feeling confident and connected is only a heartbeat away. You won't believe how easy it is to neutralize strong emotions. No need to avoid them or try and make them go away... No complicated breathing techniques... No requirement for meditation or other distractions for the mind. Just understanding how your brain works, then utilize that knowledge.

Let me start by explaining The Switching Technique.

What is The Switching Technique?

The Switching Technique is the natural switching which occurs between the conscious mind and the subconscious mind. This switching enables the person to be separately in either part of the mind but not in both parts simultaneously.

There are many spheres and components which make the brain operate but essentially for yourself, you just need to know about these two: The Conscious Mind and the Subconscious Mind. For explanation sake, I have used these descriptions so any person reading this will understand more easily than the technical terms.

These brain sections and their functions have been hotly debated over the years by many psychologists, philosophers, and scientists, because it's very hard to empirically prove they exist. Despite all this, I find it a great analogy to use and at the end of the day if it works for you and makes sense, then that's all that matters.

The Conscious Mind is the reasoning, analytical and logical part of your brain. It's constantly reasoning and calculating ALL information given to it. This information generally enters through your senses – via sight, smell, hearing, taste and touch. Usually this analysis is to determine the facts - what is false or true? What you want or what you don't want? It also makes the decision to perform a task then selects the appropriate muscle program from the subconscious mind to perform the appropriate action.

Whereas the Subconscious Mind is like a storage facility which stores all that incoming information as facts and memories. It also contains the programs for your body functions. Due to its ability to store massive amounts of data and to "remember" new programs, your subconscious mind is far more powerful than your conscious mind. Just like a computer, your conscious mind "switches" to access the data and programs stored in your subconscious mind.

You are switching all day, every day. Here's an example of how the switching works. If someone is speaking to you while they ask you to read a document, your attention will switch from one to the other. From listening to reading, then back again. But you can't focus fully on both at the same time. When you start listening, you stop reading. When you start reading, you stop listening. These are two completely different programs and you can only focus on one at a time.

Some people have the mental dexterity to be able to rapidly switch between listening and reading. Although it's important for them to note that there will still be discrepancies in what was said and what was remembered. This is due to words being missed when thinking about what was being read before switching back into listening mode.

If you give your full attention to what the person is saying you cannot take in what you are reading. And this happens in reverse. You cannot do justice to either task because you cannot give your full attention to both at the same time. And if you're trying to focus on one, the other quickly becomes an annoying distraction!

This also happens when someone is speaking to us. Instead of fully listening, we are thinking about what we are going to say in reply. This is where many errors in communication take place, why arguments result - and why so many people feel unheard and misunderstood! This is why statistically people only remember 20% of a conversation. Remember that your mind can only focus on one thing at a time.

Switching also naturally occurs as you switch your attention from a thought to an action... or from one task to another. Such as switching from braking to accelerating when you are driving a car.

Although it's normal for your mind to lose direction and wander with random thoughts, this can have dire consequences during tasks such as driving or other operations which require your attention such as sex. This is because your conscious mind can only focus on one task at a time. You may be familiar with this concept if you ever tried to text on your phone while driving!

Mistakes happen when your mind wanders, you stop paying attention and you don't correct your focus as required. During any task, you need to reorganize your thoughts to ensure you keep the correct focal sequence and activate the correct muscle programs attached to that or those thoughts.

CONTROL your thoughts and correctly realign your actions so you don't physically lose control over your task. This is the beginning of self-control.

This can also apply to mental and emotional conflict. When we're not paying attention to our thoughts (and where we're allowing those thoughts to take us) we can quickly spiral down through a negative thought process which will constantly trigger anxiety and other strong emotions and may eventually result in depression.

Ilow Our "Programs" Develop

As a young child, we learned how to walk from crawling... and how to eat using utensils. Unlike other common human requirements, with these programs we generally receive a great deal of instruction and guidance. For example, during the formative years the brain works out the programs for the muscles. It learns to utilize the growing muscles and develop the skill level of using those muscles to a higher degree of control.

Each program includes:
Balance - Position – Limitations

The programs you learn, and all your life memories are labelled, stored and contained in your subconscious (which is like a massive warehouse) and accessed by a keyword - a thought. Your conscious mind identifies a need via a thought then it switches into the subconscious and plucks out the relevant stored information and program. If you don't have a sequentially logical program stored you're going to have problems and emotional resistance is going to be triggered!

Your conscious mind makes a decision based on all of the options and choices it has from information it has considered from within the subconscious part of the brain. Then it switches to the subconscious mind for the programs and muscle actions for those programs.

Generally, we're taught specific procedures for most tasks. This makes it easy for our brain to switch to the ideal program pre-determined by our conscious mind.

But what if you don't have an ideal program? What if the task is something you haven't specifically been taught? What if you've attempted the task in the past but the experience didn't turn out well?

This commonly occurs with sex. We're not taught a specific start to end thought and action procedure for sex (the mental mechanics) in our sex education. Therefore, we have no idea what sequence we're supposed to be following. This causes our brain to become confused and frustrated as to which muscle program we want. This is what happened to the Doctor in my reference section!

When your mind is confused (or distracted) during any external activity, it's generally because you don't have a complete start to end procedure for that activity stored in your brain.

... Or because you're indulging in random thoughts.

... Or because you're unsure of the correct procedure.

... Or because you're not paying attention and you switch to the wrong subject or task which results in confusing your brain with mixed signals and incorrect information.

It's normal to default to panic when you don't know what to focus on or what to switch your focus onto. When we're not totally sure of a procedure it triggers anxiety and/or other intense emotional responses. If the emotional response is unresolved this can then animate the wrong muscle program.

Paul told me that one night while he was playing in a snooker room, there was a loud *SMASH* outside. He ran out the door and found a car imbedded in a public toilet in the adjacent carpark. After checking that the driver was alright he asked how it happened. The driver was practicing driving around the carpark when he bent down to look at the pedals and stood on the accelerator instead of the clutch. Go instead of stop. The toilet had to be completely rebuilt.

Another problem we encounter is when we don't understand the sequence required for an emotional response to complete. We can become further distracted and can inadvertently launch our mind into a confused tangle of negative thinking.

The common mismatch during an emotional response is having confusion contaminate the process. As adult human beings, we have been indoctrinated and interrupted since childhood to think about our actions. To think about what is happening. To think about what we should be doing or saying. To think about what someone else is saying. And to think about why we're feeling that way. Unfortunately, we never resolve our own thoughts - only theirs, which leads us to over-thinking and analysis paralysis – which then trigger further emotional chaos!

To feel calm and connected we need to resolve these negative thought processes. The fastest way to do this is to briefly "switch" our attention to allow the brief physical discomfort of the emotional response to pass. Just like we do when we feel a sneeze coming on. We momentarily pause whatever we were focusing on and switch our attention to allow the sneeze to pass. We're just allowing that uncomfortable moment in time to pass also.

By doing this, we automatically switch from the constant analysis of the conscious mind into our subconscious mind. And as we switch into our subconscious mind during the emotional response, we automatically initiate the programs which regulate our breathing, our heart rate, our blood pressure and relaxes our muscles. THIS is what makes us instantly start feeling better and relieves the pressure from the emotional response!

Doing this ONE thing enables you to feel better every time an emotional response has been triggered! Anger, frustration, fear, disgust; now you can begin to neutralize ANY emotion to start feeling peaceful and connected!

Understanding Depression, Resistance and The Emotional Response

Resistance is that uncomfortable, clenched fist, bated breath, sinking kind of a feeling. We experience it when something goes wrong such as losing sight of a small child. Or when someone says something we don't like, or we have to do something we disagree with. We often feel this way when we are facing a situation which has triggered previously repressed thoughts or feelings and is challenging us.

It is the physical feeling we experience before we have thoughts about it. Whatever the trigger is, the feeling of resistance is distinctly uncomfortable. It's those moments in time when we feel an instant mental, emotional and physical disconnect from being in the flow with ourselves and others and is the moment we immediately feel separated.

The definition of resistance in the dictionary is: your opposition to an attempt to bring repressed thoughts or feelings into consciousness. Opposition is the key word here. Resistance is like the repelling force of two similar poles of two powerful magnets coming together. When you're in a state of resisting your current situation, it's as if you're pushing to move past that feeling in an attempt to ignore it. However, that has a repelling effect on your mind which causes your mind to further resist by engaging in a mental debate and dialogue:

Oh no, what if this happens? What if that happens? What will I do if I can't find the answer? Why do I have this problem? Why can't I solve this problem? Why is life so hard? What's wrong with me? Why can't I get this to work?? Grrrrrrr.

You then have the opposition effect happening. It's like dialing in between two radio stations and only getting the static. You're fighting the feeling (of the sense of inadequacy) and then pushing back with your mind. You don't feel calm nor can you think clearly when you are in this resistant state. From an operational perspective, this creates a frustrating degree of mental and emotional chaos.

I believe that many instances of depression are caused by constantly analyzing everyone and every related or unrelated situation with your mind which then triggers resistance, other uncomfortable emotional responses and self-doubt about your ability. Especially when you don't have the required skills to pull yourself up when your thoughts start spiraling out of control. The ensuing analysis paralysis leads you to some pretty depressing and judgmental thoughts - about yourself, about others; and how empty and alone you think you feel.

Every time you stop yourself from experiencing the brief physical discomfort related to an emotional response, it prevents you from untangling the emotional issue which will surely follow. But they don't teach you this at school. Teenagers often feel overwhelmed and unprepared when hormonal responses are added to the mix.

Then there are all those unwanted negative emotional responses – we describe them as anger, frustration, sadness, disappointment, fear and anxiety, which when left unmanaged can make you feel totally isolated, depressed... disconnected, frustrated AND alone.

This malady doesn't suddenly disappear with age. Thoughts and the related emotional responses are constant, they must be managed. If they're not managed, then you automatically become needy of an external feeling fix such as Russell with his gambling - someone or something to make you feel better. But as you've already discovered in life, there is nothing outside of you which ever gives you any sense of lasting satisfaction.

You think everyone else has it all together - everyone else SEEMS to be happy. At least, they're obviously not as bad off as you are. Constantly thinking this way and over-analyzing makes you feel worse until you feel totally paralyzed by your own thoughts. It seems like you just can't get yourself away from those crazy imaginings which could lead to a downward spiral.

Back and forth your mind goes [playing mental table tennis] – past to future, past to future.

Imagining the worst... not seeing an answer to your problem... imagining that no-one understands you... imagining that you are too broken to be fixed... The more time you spend in your mind analyzing why you think you feel that way, the more disconnected and desolate you will feel.

How many times do you worry about what someone else is thinking of you? You get stuck thinking about past scenarios with other people. Yet, most people are so busy with mental chaos in their own lives, they've already forgotten a previous misunderstanding or words which you think they may have misconstrued and misunderstood.

However, the more *you* think about it, the worse your imagined scenarios become until you have completely overwhelmed yourself. In most cases, it's your mind's crazy imaginings which are keeping you depressed or stuck in thoughts of not being good enough. You can only try for so long to be (and feel) something that you are not. The intensity of those uncomfortable-feeling emotional responses can appear to be overwhelming. Because of that, you keep stopping yourself from feeling them – which keeps you stuck in your conscious mind constantly analyzing why your piece of life's puzzle doesn't seem to fit.

I can relate to this, it used to be me. I was so messed up when I was a teen and then later after Russell died. I felt like I was on a mental and emotional roller coaster which never seemed to end. It was horrible. For that earlier part of my life I felt isolated and alone, I felt totally disconnected. I felt like I was on the outside of life looking in; not really fitting in anywhere. I was constantly searching for that elusive "something" which would make me feel better, something which would make me feel complete. I had heard about loving myself, but I had no idea how to do it.

I didn't know that I was the master of my own destiny – or that I could be if I chose to be. Instead, I was constantly the victim of my own thoughts, stuck in an endless maze of memories of pain and fearsome imaginings of being alone in the future.

Because I was constantly resisting the physical discomfort related to an emotional response, by default I was resistant to experiencing life as it could be. Locked within the cage of my mind I cycled through thoughts of judgment, blame, self-pity and resentment.

I had a constant feeling of resistance. The more I tried to escape from my own feelings of resistance, the more resistant others became towards me. I never seemed to feel heard. Nobody seemed to understand me. However, it was my own resistant behavior which was pushing others away from me. The constant related emotional responses were overwhelming. I was continuously seeking solace from my thoughts and the related emotions.

At the height of my teenage years while I was experiencing my separation from reality, it led me into a state of depression. I was aware that I was segregating myself and choosing to be a victim. Yet, I was constantly judging others for my own feelings of disconnection. I felt lonely and it seemed like I would never feel like I belonged anywhere. My mind was constantly blaming everyone and everything for the cause of my own misery. I did not take responsibility for my own inaction.

As emotional human beings, we can become so used to shutting down the uncomfortable feelings of the emotional response that we become constantly trapped in the judgments of our own mind. Then we analyze why we aren't good enough, why we don't fit in, and why we don't feel worthy.

We can begin to imagine that no-one likes us, no-one understands us, and no-one will even notice if we are gone... We can start thinking thoughts like, "I just feel so sad and it's so *hard* to be me... Nobody gets me. Nobody understands how I feel... I don't want to be here anymore... I feel so alone..." On and on, our mind commiserates about how miserable we are – until those depressing thoughts obsessively fill our mind.

The more we focus on how bad it is, the worse it seems to get. It seems like the whole world is conspiring to make us feel miserable. We anticipate feeling bad and we resist kind and well-intended comments from everyone, insisting to remain in our mind's version of how separate and alone we are.

In my opinion, many instances of depression are caused by the mind being trapped in a negative thinking cycle of judgment, blame, self-pity and resentment. When you blame a person or a situation for how you feel; you remain stuck in your own pity party and then you feel totally trapped in a self-imposed resistant state.

Many people who suffer from depression have shut themselves down from allowing the physical discomfort of an emotional response because the initial intensity of it seems overwhelming. When you're feeling bad, you're feeling really bad and no-one wants to feel worse, right?

Addictions are Emotional Feeling Fixes

There are no amounts of alcohol, drugs, cigarettes or any other external feeling fix which can turn off the endless recriminations fabricated in our own mind. While we may try and convince ourselves that we're just having a couple of drinks to relax, in reality we start with a couple of drinks to escape from our thoughts and the demands on our life. But our mind never stops thinking, remembering, judging and condemning, so we keep drinking.

It's interesting to observe that there is no-one and no-thing which can make us feel completely connected. Sure, doing some-thing or connecting with someone may make it seem like we are improving inwardly - for a brief time. But do you notice that it is short-lived?

You have those words from someone or an indulgence in something... It may be a drink, or a smoke, or a drug, or a shopping trip, or a trip to the refrigerator... or sex, or a partner who usually doesn't treat you right but is sometimes nice. Something that takes you temporarily into *feeling* intensely present – even if just for a moment.

> David was just 19 years old when he was referred to me to solve his sexual dysfunction problem. Upon further questioning of him, he mentioned that he was also trying to give up smoking but couldn't get past his great

emotional need to have a cigarette. In the past, he had been sent to counselling after being caught smoking marijuana. He described that drug as being the only thing which made him feel good as a person. When that option was taken away from him, he wondered at the craziness of it and had said to his parents, "You mean you're taking away from me the only thing which makes me feel good and makes me want to live?"

For me when I was a teen, it was smoking, it was alcohol, or it was someone being nice to me. I lived for those moments. Even just the thought of having one of those things would make me start feeling better. But these were fabricated outside of me which meant I was always on a continuous search for more external fixes. I was totally dependent on my external "fixes" to make myself feel better as a person. At that time, I didn't have the skills or knowledge to feel totally connected within myself.

What's your external feeling fix, that you use to take yourself into that zone of feeling good?

One of the most common feeling fixes is morning coffee. You put the kettle on, put your mug on the benchtop and add your essential ingredients. As you wait for the kettle to boil you do other tasks – but part of you is already anticipating how you are going to feeeeeeel gooooood when you have that hot drink.

Finally, your other tasks are completed – it's coffee time! (or tea, or whatever). You sit yourself down with the steaming mug of your favorite morning hot drink fixed firmly between your hands. Already you have immersed yourself into the associated sensations...

You have the first sip - the first initial rush of feeling hits you. Ahhhhhhhhh... that feels soooooooo good... However, on your second sip you begin to *think* about how good that felt but as soon as you start thinking, poof! You're no longer aware of any sensations. Your mind begins to analyze the busyness of your day ahead, contemplating problems and searching for possible answers and solutions.

You go to take another sip - but your cup is already empty! (And you only remember having the first two sips!) Your mind had become so immersed in thinking about the day that you had totally lost the awareness of the delicious sensations in your body. Every coffee you have thereafter is a disappointment in comparison to how good the first sip from the initial cup made you feel.

This is what it's like for those who indulge in alcohol. You just keep having another drink and another drink, trying to replicate the effects of that first drink, hoping to regain that initial rush and to feel better once more.

What if you are a smoker? Your first cigarette of the day... again, you are busily preparing yourself for the day ahead... anticipating the feeling of the puff of your first cigarette of the day... Much like the liquid feeling fix, you have your first puff... as you breathe in; you feeeeeeeeel the sensations of that inhalation – from head to toe.

Then you start thinking about your day ahead. Before you know it, your cigarette has burned down to the filter and you're reaching for another one, trying to recreate that initial relaxed feeling buzz which you experienced with the first hit. But this cigarette doesn't have anywhere near the same effect as the first one. Nor do any of the ensuing cigarettes you smoke – unless you set up the anticipation of how good it is going to feel when you have that next smoke!

As humans, we commonly decide that when we have this (something or someone) we will feel better. We are *so* looking forward to the feeling this 'thing' will bring us. Soon after that initial 'hit' (of that someone or something) we start thinking about how good that feels. But that awareness of feeling is only a temporary point of focus and within seconds it dissipates and vanishes.

Generally, you can think in a relaxed manner for about 10 seconds before your mind switches into its regular, analytical "fix it, solve it, find answers" mode.

As soon as your mind begins its endless search for solutions and answers to your problems, you immediately start losing that feeling of connection. So, what do you do? You reach for another 'hit' of that external something (or someone) to make yourself feel better again.

Eventually, it just doesn't seem to work at all because you have moved back into a thinking analysis when you switched yourself out from the awareness of feeling. While it appears that you are following through with the same actions, you have already switched back into thinking a constant stream of thoughts instead of simply enjoying those delicious sensations within yourself. This induces that feeling of connection to evaporate within a few short seconds.

The reason that it felt so amazingly good was simply because you were completely focused on enjoying the sensations within your body. Your mind can only focus on one thing at a time and *you* were focusing on enjoying your sensations.

That first puff or drink or 'hit' takes you into an intense awareness of sensations. And it FEELS GOOD. Then what happens? You associate that thing outside of yourself as the thing that made you feel better. Duh.

That was my sequence for a really long time, in fact many years. Because I simply didn't know how to manufacture "feeling good as a person".

Sometimes we become totally obsessed with thinking about our problems. In this case we will feel worse; irrespective of what day it is or whatever else we are doing. How many times do you arrange to go on a holiday only to find that when you get there your mind is so busy that you can hardly relax. Then you need to reach for another feeling fix such as food or alcohol to make yourself feel better?

You take your mind with you wherever you go. Now knowing that your mind will always be busy analyzing stuff, you need to balance this by allowing every emotional response to pass. Because if you never do this one thing, your mind will never ever rest. And if your mind is not resting then your body will never completely relax either.

This is the reason why, so many people become overwhelmed with everyday living. There's always so much to do and so many things which require their attention. When they don't switch to allow the physical discomfort of an emotional response to pass, their brain goes into overdrive. This burns a heck of a lot of energy and will leave you feeling depleted, emotionally as well as physically. Remember that your brain is only 2% of your body weight yet uses 20% of your energy.

It can be difficult to give up an external feeling fix without first knowing how to replicate that feeling good sensation within yourself once more. This is why so many people swap one addiction for another. They stop smoking and start eating. Stop alcohol and start or increase drug intake. Until you understand the correlation between feeling emotional and mentally good, you will continue to be at the mercy of such substances or outside influences.

In my previous example, David had to give up smoking pot, so he took up smoking cigarettes. It was only after I taught him the sequence for how to deal with a triggered emotional response that he was immediately able to quit smoking without suffering any mental duress. He no longer felt the need for alcohol. And with the advanced knowledge his brain needed, he regained full sexual function as well. He said that I had provided him with more relevant knowledge and skills within a few sessions than all the combined years of counselling which he had attended up to that point.

Some people give up all their external feeling fixes however they never give up their need to control others. This alternate "fix" plays out a lot in relationships. When we feel emotionally out of control ourselves (which makes it impossible to clearly communicate our needs) it's a natural inclination to try and influence others because *we* want to better understand this mystery!

How to Allow an Emotional Response to Pass (With the Ease of a Sneeze)

Not all emotions feel bad – which is why we often find ourselves chasing the "good" emotions such as feelings of love, peace, happiness and joy. These emotions feel physically uplifting, they feel good and that's why we want to experience more of them!

Whereas "bad" emotions such as anxiety, fear, disappointment, frustration and anger feel intensely uncomfortable within our body. These emotions feel heavy like they are weighing us down. And we want to feel better – not worse, so we try to switch our attention away from this physical discomfort. But that's what keeps us feeling emotionally and mentally trapped.

Physically, "good" or "bad" emotional response programs usually only last for a few seconds – just like a sneeze. That's why feelings of love, peace and joy are so fleeting because they're part of your in-built emotional response program!

While experiencing "negative" emotions it's a simple process of switching your attention so you are allowing the brief, physical discomfort related to that emotional response. Usually you try not to feel the discomfort of emotions because it's intense! And it's uncomfortable. However, as soon as you switch your attention to allow the discomfort to be there, it's immediately gone... just like the brief discomfort of a sneeze. It's there one moment then gone in the next.

Have you ever tried to stop a sneeze? If you have, you know that it's not a good idea as the suppressed force can physically hurt you. Generally, when you feel the discomfort of a sneeze coming on, what do you do? Do you try to ignore it? Do you try to make it go away? Do you analyze it? No, you simply brace yourself and allow the sneeze to be executed. Then you get on with whatever you were doing. While a sneeze is a more violent physical response program than the emotional response, it starts off the same way:

Aaaaaaaaah (you're noticing the mental, physical or emotional discomfort of the triggered emotional response) Chooooooo! You briefly switch your attention to allow the physical discomfort of it to happen and within a second of making that switch, the discomfort has already passed.

From now on any strong emotion can be just a moment in time which passes because you allowed it. When we prevent the emotional response program from completing (by trying *not* to feel the physical discomfort of it) it's like stepping on a bear trap concealed in the grass.

However, every emotional response ends in a feeling of peace, in completion of that briefly intense program. This physical, mental and emotional peace lasts only for a few fleeting moments but built up over the course of a day, many emotional responses can result in many moments of peace. In the same instance, many emotional suppressed moments can add up to a huge amount of anxiety, frustration or related emotions.

So, throughout the course of the day you can continually feel better – instead of just waiting for those elusive happy moments in life to find you. They will be very few and far between if you interrupt them!

"BAD" EMOTIONS >>> BRIEFLY SWITCH TO SENSATIONS >>> PEACE

"GOOD" EMOTIONS >>> BRIEFLY SWITCH TO SENSATIONS >>> PEACE

When you think about it, you're always seeking experiences which make you feel good! Yet, every emotion *allows* you to feel good at the *end* of the physical response.

Before the thoughts of anxiety or other unwanted emotions is the physical discomfort of the emotional response which is a momentary sensation of discomfort or a sense of disconnect. The physical emotional response always takes place first. It feels like a wave of intense discomfort such as increased heart rate and muscle tension. This physical discomfort or sense of disconnection precedes the thoughts about why you think you feel this way.

Then if you try to ignore that brief wave of physical discomfort you will automatically switch (by nature of how your brain works) to the million negative thoughts which are related to that issue. Because you can only be in your conscious mind or your subconscious mind at any one time, if you ignore the emotional response, then you will automatically default back to your conscious mind and start re-analyzing all the thoughts which triggered the initial response. And that's what causes the downward spiral and makes you feel unsure about yourself or how to resolve the issue.

What usually happens is when an emotional response is triggered, you try not to feel that way. Then you start thinking negatively... and when you realize this... ANOTHER emotional response is triggered. If you resist *that* emotional response you will switch back into more negative thoughts. It's like a:

SWITCH >>> SWITCH >>> SWITCH

WRONG REACTION:
Emotional response - switch to negative thought - switch to emotional response - switch to negative thought - switch to emotional response. This becomes an endless loop.

It doesn't matter if or when you recognize you're having negative thoughts or an emotional response As long as when you do, you realize that you're in a state of disconnection. This can be recognized by feeling out of sync emotionally, mentally or physically - and you just can't think clearly. You then need to SWITCH to allow that brief moment of physical discomfort related to that emotional response to just be.

Don't tell yourself not to think about it because that will make you think about it more intensely. Stop fighting the physical discomfort of it and the discomfort is immediately reduced to nothing. Don't focus your attention on the sensations, it's just a momentary interruption in that moment of time. As soon as you stop fighting yourself, you naturally relax. You don't have to think about relaxing because feeling relaxed is the natural result of doing this one thing.

If you purposely slow your breathing down, then you're drawing your attention to *that* action. Whereas when you stop fighting and allow the moment of the discomfort related to the emotional response, as you switch to allow *that* moment you also activate the programs which regulate your breathing, blood pressure, heart rate and relax your muscles. For sure, this will make you feel better. The emotional response program interrupts these programs which is what causes the initial discomfort.

You're not allocating those thoughts any attention and you're not giving the physical discomfort any consideration. If you try to exaggerate the feeling and feel it "more intensely," you're bringing your full attention to the sensations and generating more of them.

When you initially notice the anxiety or any emotional response, that's when the "feeling" is most intense. And as you allow that moment of intense discomfort (you stop fighting it) it immediately reduces to nothing. You're just allowing that uncomfortable moment in time to pass with the ease of a sneeze:

SWITCH >>> SWITCH >>> SWITCH

RIGHT RESPONSE:
Emotional response - switch to allow the brief wave of sensation to happen - then switch to correct your focus to a more empowering point of view. "Things always work out for me, I can *do* this." Now you're switching your focus toward the solution.

Your mind will always fill the void at the end of the emotional response so it's up to you to control the direction of those thoughts. If you don't move to more empowering thoughts, then you may default back to a habitual point of focus.

THINK OF IT AS:

Assessing *your own* reaction (anxiety, negative thoughts, whatever they are) ... Allowing *that* brief discomfort (realize and switch to allow it, instead of fighting it or analyzing it) ... Just breathe normally... Switch your attention to... passively allowing this chain of events to naturally occur so you can continue what you were doing without disruption.

When you try to think about reformulating without *first allowing* the emotional response to resolve, you're still disconnected from the resolution which will liberate you from uncertainty. This uncertainty feels like mental chaos as your mind is jumping all over the place desperately trying to resolve the issue. And you can't think clearly.

It's just a brief moment of physical discomfort OR if you try to ignore it, it's the million negative thoughts about everything associated with it. Emotion can't be controlled just like a sneeze can't be controlled but you can let them both pass and be resolved.

Letting go doesn't mean analyzing your thoughts or sensations, it's just allowing the discomfort of that brief moment in time to resolve with the ease of a sneeze. If you over analyze the physical discomfort of resistance, your mind will return to your thoughts about it.

Nearly every emotional response completes within seconds. This is why you haven't been able to "pause" it if you've been trying to "let it go". When you're trying to pause it, you keep recycling through more negative thoughts which then trigger more emotional responses!

Regardless of the label you have previously put on the emotion you are facing, when you switch your attention to allow the brief physical discomfort (instead of fighting it) you immediately enable yourself to feel better.

Begin now by becoming more aware of any time you are feeling out of sorts emotionally, mentally or physically. And instead of fighting the discomfort of it, just allow that brief moment to happen. In doing this, you will be practicing allowing an emotional response to pass with the ease of a sneeze.

The emotional response is a naturally occurring program like a yawn and a sneeze. The moment you stop fighting it is the moment it resolves.

Emotions and Problems: The Chicken or the Egg?

Allowing yourself to worry about what might or might not happen next is the most common cause of negative emotional responses. These may include anxiety, fear, anger and frustration as well as their related problems. It doesn't matter what your problem is – if you don't know how to solve it, anxiety and other strong emotions will constantly be triggered.

This is also frequently experienced by those who have suffered from sexual abuse and or are currently suffering from sexual dysfunction problems. It's common for the one problem to lead to another when we overthink the possible correlation between the past and future experiences.

Why do I use sexual abuse as an example? Because sexual abuse is prevalent in society and detrimentally affects the lives of all involved. This includes the victim, his or her family and friends, future partners, children and even employers and work colleagues. Everyone is affected when the post traumatic effects of the abuse continue.

I also use this example because many men and women who have been sexually abused inadvertently continue being victimized by their own thoughts. This isn't done on purpose, it's just a by-product of second-guessing both themselves and their future.

This of course, leads to more emotional responses being triggered!

Continuing with the example of sexual abuse, let's examine the reality of why I was previously finding it difficult to achieve orgasm years after the abuse had ended:

I was constantly worrying about my inability to achieve orgasm and surmising that it was the sexual abuse which caused that problem. I wasn't allowing emotional responses to pass whenever they were triggered by those thoughts or switching to enjoy having sex. This resulted in confusing my brain during sex.

I had never learned a complete start to end procedure for sex, so I was constantly distracted by analysis paralysis such as, "Is it? Is it? Is it?" when it started to feel good... This distracted me from uploading an effective experiential orgasm program in my brain. I had no understanding of what an orgasm was supposed to feel like nor did I know what my brain required from me to achieve an orgasm during sex.

This kept me cycling through disempowering thoughts which triggered emotional responses... Then more negative thoughts which resulted in further emotional responses... and that depressing cycle continued for many years.

How was my brain supposed to know which muscle program I wanted? I hadn't given my brain the correct information, sequence and program to initiate (and complete) the orgasm program. My random thoughts and lack of relevant information were in fact, confusing my brain!

When emotional responses are being triggered back to back due to constant over-thinking, it's impossible to access any state of emotional or physical fulfilment in that present moment. This is because our thoughts have wandered from an action to an unrelated "inactive" thought and are constantly analyzing what happened in the past and what might happen in the future. There is total confusion about which program your brain should be using!

And when it comes to solving challenges such as sex problems, you need to be present and paying attention to providing the signals that your brain needs to achieve success in those tasks! Our brain runs on procedures and if you don't have a good start to end procedure for a task, anxiety or other strong emotions will be triggered and will divert your attention away from your goal. This is normal.

> Anything we're learning that is new can cause us to experience anxiety
> Not knowing how to solve a problem can cause us to experience anxiety and other strong emotions
> Any subject that we don't know enough about can cause us to experience anxiety

> ➤ An incorrect procedure which confuses our brain will cause us to experience anxiety

> ➤ Random, negative thought sequences will also trigger anxiety and other emotional responses

> ➤ Random events which directly affect us and appear out of our control will most certainly trigger emotional responses

We're HUMAN. And as humans we experience emotional responses 40+ times per day – and that's on a good day! Emotional responses are NORMAL.

In our earlier years, it wasn't our choice to suppress our emotions. This course of action was chosen for us either by our parents or by well-meaning teachers or other adults. Then it became habitual to continue doing so. As we continued with this completely ineffectual procedure to deal with our emotions, we inadvertently set up a new (and grossly ineffective) program in our brain.

This meant that instead of simply allowing an emotional response to happen with the ease of a sneeze, we created a new default setting - which was to start thinking about why we thought we felt that way! This happened because we were always told to stop or delay the physical reaction of an emotional response, which by default switched us back to the thinking process.

Example: if we felt elated in the classroom for any reason, we were told to wait until lunch time to express it. How is that supposed to work? Delay our reactions for two hours?? That's not normal!

Have you ever wondered why life sometimes seems so devoid of emotions as an adult? This has developed from when you were a child, from when you continually tried to stop yourself from feeling upset, or angry, or frustrated.

Because of the natural switching which occurs in our brain we cannot focus on thinking and feeling at the same time. By switching out of one, we automatically switch to the other.

Most people want to feel better but don't know how. Our strong emotions tend to regenerate every-one else's repressed feelings. This triggers an emotional response in them also, which makes them act resistant towards us. Due to this, we all try and shut our emotions down and try not to think about feeling that way in a vain attempt to stay connected with others. But this doesn't work and makes us start feeling disconnected from ourselves and out of sync. This results in it becoming even more difficult for us to communicate clearly; which then affects our ability to feel heard.

Remember that the subconscious contains ALL of your memories and stores them as data. As you become older you can then access a huge database of memories related to specific emotions which means that you can spend hours analyzing why you might be feeling a particular way.

Another problem with waging a constant mental battle within yourself is that it's impossible for your body to relax. The programs which regulate your breathing, heart rate, blood pressure, and relax your muscles cannot be maintained in tandem with a stressful thought sequence.

Constantly thinking about a problem causes you to retrigger the associated emotions and overwhelm yourself with your imagined outcomes. You then start avoiding feeling the emotions in the hope that will make you feel better. Unfortunately, that doesn't happen because it's not how your brain works.

Your conscious mind is constantly analyzing all the information given to it. So, what happens when you're constantly dredging up a past issue – what you did wrong, what you wish you had done differently, how the person reacted, etc, then you are predominantly going to be focused on self-inflicted pain and problems. This will trigger more emotional responses... which you will then try not to feel. This then makes your cycle of self-destruction continue.

Adults generally have a difficult time dealing with intense emotions whether they are their own or someone else's. This is because strong emotions tend to add to layers of previously incompletely ful-

filled emotional feelings which have not been resolved and completed.

That's the reason why, when a person starts arguing with you they tend to bring up unresolved issues
from the past – and all the repressed emotions associated with those events! Then those associated
emotions (and related emotional responses) are
again experienced by that person in that present
moment.

*Resistant feelings suppressed for years will always re-
surface if they haven't been dealt with. The logical way
to effectively deal with emotions and previously resisted
feelings is to allow them to resolve as they become triggered.*

When it feels uncomfortable mentally, physically or
emotionally, it's a clear indicator that an emotional
response has been triggered. If you choose to continue to ignore the physical discomfort of an emotional response, your mind will continue cycling and
recycling through all your associated issues from the
past and whatever is happening at present. This ac-
cumulated effect will begin to imagine future problems.

How many times do you have imaginary conversations with people? Remembering conversations
from the past and then continuing the conversation
on now in your imagination?

Why Arguing Your Point NEVER Works & the Best Way to Immediately Stop ANY Argument!

When people argue they generally use a lot of words to emphasize what they were simply experiencing as a resistant state just a moment before. However, both parties quickly become engrossed in trying to defend their own point of view.

This happens because your thoughts can take you away from the present uncomfortable feeling of an emotional response – and back into remembered (or imagined) pain and problems. You both push your point. You both want to feel heard. You both want to conclude the matter, so you can return to being in a calmer state of mind and body.

But you're too focused on pushing forwards your own perspective. Expressing all those past hurts which you never terminated when they were initially triggered. Instead of switching your attention to allow the intense physical sensations of the emotional response, your indignant reaction and conclusions from past experiences continue to build in intensity. You never get to resolve the current issue because you become entangled in a debate about the past!

Generally, before you engage in an argument with someone you're already feeling somewhat frustrated with what's going on in your life. Unresolved issues can make you feel frustrated, angry, annoyed or resentful. They can also make you feel fearful in such a way that you second guess yourself and doubt your own ability to move forward. This will also trigger anxiety! If this continues, it will lead you into a sense of feeling inadequate, overwhelmed or alone.

Life is already triggering you. You're just waiting for an "opening" so you can let steam off! The thing is – you were already feeling this way before you started arguing. These past intense feelings have been repressed by you so now they have been re-triggered by someone else or yet another challenging situation.

When you allow resistant feelings to build up throughout any period of time, anyone or anything can and will trigger you. Someone can say something quite innocently, a comment or a question which you quickly take offense to.

How often does your mind hold onto a thought of blame or resentment over something someone else has said? Instead of allowing the physical sensations of the emotional response, your mind holds onto that one statement and mentally rips it to shreds. That one thing which was said to you, brings up all those other suppressed resistant feelings of GRRRR! It's times like these anyone and every other slightly challenging situation can retrigger those previously repressed emotions.

Whatever is being said to you during an argument, understand that it's an accumulation of hurts, not just the current situation which has been triggered in the other person as well as yourself. This is why it's SO important to deal with problems (and emotional responses) as they arise, instead of ignoring them and hoping they'll go away!

So often we hear a person request a change and we think to ourselves, "Oh. It can't be all that important, they've only mentioned it once." And then we have the audacity to ignore that person's request. If anyone mentions an issue to you, I can guarantee they've thought about it and analyzed it multiple times, probably close to one hundred times. However, it's only in this moment that this person has decided (or had the courage) to communicate it to you out loud.

How many times have you felt frustrated because you've communicated something important to someone and they ignored it? How frustrating and demoralizing it feels because it seems that the other person doesn't care how much that issue annoys or bothers you, so you don't feel heard?

This is the beginning of the end for many relationships. We assume there isn't a real problem due to the lack of communication and emphasis over it. But if we're honest with ourselves we can sense that something hasn't been quite right with that other person. However, when we train ourselves to ignore an emotional response we tend to avoid conversations which could result in one. This means that in our resistance to dealing with the problem, we ignore the situation and hope the problem will melt away by itself.

Emotion has an energy, a vibration which is felt by others. Even if you think you are saying all the right words, others won't feel aligned with you because of this underlying feeling of resistance. We respond faster to a person's vibration than we respond to their words or actions.

You can sense it when someone isn't telling you the truth. Never say you are feeling ok when you are in fact upset or angry. This will make you feel even more disconnected and alone because this very action keeps you isolated from the truth and the moment at hand.

How many times have you known when people have been arguing just as you walked into a room? They're both wearing a smile on their faces and pretending that everything is ok. You can sense that something isn't quite right because of the underlying tension or friction in the air. This tension is enough to make the hairs on your neck stand up sharply!

When you feel angry about a matter and you are pretending (and saying) that everything is ok; nobody will believe you. You won't feel heard nor will you be able to feel connected. Because you are in a state of resistance this means you're out of sync with yourself. You also automatically fall out of sync with others. This is frustrating for all concerned.

If there's one thing you need to allow when an argument begins, it's what the other person needs to express. They're just as triggered as you are which means that they're probably going to say a whole lot of stuff which they will regret later. So, don't even try responding and save yourself from that additional stress.

They have felt unheard and misunderstood for a period of time and they have quite simply had enough. You just happen to be the lucky person who's in their firing line. Perhaps we put ourselves in this position, so we can offload too? A point worth considering.

When you find yourself reacting to whatever anyone else is saying, there will be intense, uncomfortable sensations of resistance going off in your body. If you try to ignore these sensations, they will become more intense and make it impossible to think logically.

It's common to become argumentative and judgmental when you resist the sensations of an emotion when they are triggered. This then results in more tension, stress and mutual separation between two people. It's important to note that when someone is being resistant towards you, it simply means that they are in a state of emotional resistance. This may take the form of angry, condescending, sarcastic, threatening, irritable, fault-finding, bullying behavior. Whichever stance they are taking toward you it may also make you feel emotionally resistant and indignant.

It's important to note that not all bullying comes from learned behavior. One of the hidden causes of bullying develops from emotional resistance due to not understanding how to deal with one's emotions. This results in mental and emotional chaos and conflict which then leads to resistant behavior toward others. The key to solving bullying is to teach children how to be emotionally resilient and to feel good within themselves regardless of what cards life is dealing. This, in turn, will significantly reduce the number of people who bully others.

If you ignore your own emotional response during an argument or altercation you will start becoming resistant in return. This means you start taking your own resistant stance by becoming defensive and trying to explain away your actions. Then you begin being even more resistant as you try to defend yourself and your integrity which you now feel is threatened.

Yet as you try to justify yourself, the other person becomes more obstinate and resistant! This leads to further alienating the other person and making them become more resistant toward you. If you want to be heard, then you must first listen. To be able to listen objectively you must allow the physical sensations of the emotional response whenever it is triggered.

So instead of fighting those intense sensations, simply switch your attention to allow the physical discomfort while you look the other person in the eye. Increased heart rate! Muscle tension! Keep your mouth shut while you allow that moment of physical discomfort. If you voice an opinion while you are under emotional duress, you will still be mentally confused and struggle to find the words which would enable you to clearly communicate your response.

As well as enabling you to feel calm and clear within seconds when the emotional response completes, this will also enable to you to clearly understand the other person's perspective AND they will feel heard. Without the distracting chaos associated with ignoring an emotional response you won't feel the need to justify yourself. Instead, you will simply listen, calmly observe the other person's perspective and respond in a thoughtful manner.

From this stance of unconditional acceptance, every relationship issue can begin to be resolved.

This was clearly demonstrated by Henry. Initially seeking my help to solve his sex problems, Henry is a truck driver who started attending my evening personal development group. Every week he would bitterly complain about having to deal with the receptionist of a company with which his firm conducted much of their business.

He had to deliver goods there twice a day. And every time he entered the reception area he found the receptionist to be rude, sarcastic and nasty towards him. It got to the point where he was considering finding employment elsewhere just, so he wouldn't have to confront her.

As he travelled to her premises each day he would contemplate her reception of him and how nasty she would probably be. By the time he arrived, his blood would be nearly boiling with the indignance of having to deal with her!

Understanding that there was an underlying emotional resistance issue causing this, I explained to Henry how the emotional response program in his brain works. I then suggested that whenever he thought of this woman he should stop fighting that resistant feeling and allow the physical sensations of the emotional response, so they could pass unheeded. I told him that anxiety, frustration and other strong emotions can easily be resolved with the ease of a sneeze technique.

Henry started diligently applying this technique. Every time he thought of her, "the witch!" Increased heart rate! Muscle tension! Bated breath! Now, instead of fighting the physical discomfort which was triggered by thinking about her, he simply allowed that brief moment of discomfort to pass. He found that as he applied this technique, his mind stopped analyzing this woman and judging (which were to him) her obvious faults. All the recriminating judgments diminished when he started doing this one thing.

He started feeling more relaxed as he approached her office building. As if by magic, this huge source of mental stress and anxiety disappeared from within Henry. He found himself smiling at her when he dropped off his deliveries. By the end of the second day of applying this technique, they were smiling at each other. By the end of the first week they were greeting each other by name.

Last time I heard from Henry, his twice daily deliveries to that office had become the highlight of his working week.

Taking Care of Your Own Emotional Fulfilment

Let's just take a moment to reiterate this important fact. You are uniquely you. Why do you waste valuable time trying to think and be like everyone else? You have unique quirks. You have unique likes and dislikes. You have a unique personality and a unique style which as an individual you use to shape your life. This is what makes you special and the world a brighter place because of you.

Without allowing the physical discomfort of emotion to be felt, you will consistently become stuck in the thinking trap. Constantly analyzing your thoughts and your feelings related to those thoughts. Wondering if you will ever feel like you have purpose in your life. Wondering if you will ever truly feel like you belong.

An important byproduct of resolving an emotional issue is it allows you to attain a personal achievement. Achievements can be attained on any subject matter which is either emotional, mental, artistic or physical. Usually upon realizing an achievement there is the timely release of endorphins. This feel good mood elevator makes the person feel uplifted and buoyant for an extended period of time as happened in Henry's case. This is the total opposite of emotional suppression. The point of which is to try to achieve steps in your life which will elevate your mood.

Achievements are the natural focal points for success, the ending of a challenging subject, the acquisition of new skills, the realization of a dream. The choice of subjects is endless, but the end result is an intense concentration with an eye focused on achieving a result. Achieving the desired result will yield an emotional response which will pass with exhilaration and a feeling of accomplishment for excelling at living!

Without the color of emotion, it can appear like you're becoming devoid of feeling (and direction) in your life. This leads to requiring someone else – or something else - to fulfil you. I personally discovered this when I was learning my life lessons in attraction. Relying on others to make you feel fulfilled emotionally is disastrous as it leaves you perpetually in a state of wanting, waiting and needing. This requires someone else to make you feel better. To the other person involved, this often appears as a suffocating relationship which eventually has a repelling effect on them.

Besides *that* fact, how often are those other people emotionally, mentally or physically available when you most need them to be? The needier we are, the more resistance we will experience from the people we most want to connect with.

Smothering or ignoring your emotional responses causes you to go out of attraction alignment. This then causes you to lose your sense of self-worth and the joy of feeling emotionally connected and balanced. This then distracts you from taking steps to make your own life come alive or to take consistent steps to fulfil yourself as a person. This inevitably chips away from within yourself and makes you feel like you're missing out on something important. If you make the misfortunate mistake of comparing yourself to someone else, in that moment you totally lose yourself and prevent yourself from feeling connected with anyone including yourself.

When you choose to deny an emotional response from occurring, the emotion doesn't cease to exist. You simply store it along with the cause, so it can be retriggered again when you are in similar circumstances. Your subconscious mind already has a large database of stored emotions which can be randomly triggered so why add more fuel to the fire?

You are an essential piece of life's puzzle. However, when you consistently analyze your thoughts and the ensuing emotions, then your unique piece of the puzzle will never feel like it fits in anywhere. There is no feeling of peace or connection when you're in a state of mental confusion.

The more you resist your emotions, the more others will be resistant towards you. Everything in life is interconnected and suppressed emotion is always felt by the other person – even when you yourself, are trying to ignore it or hide it!

Every time you lose part of who you are (to try and fit in or to feel like you belong with someone) you then lose your unique individual personality. And that includes when you refrain from communicating what you need in your relationships with other people. I learned that fact the hard way which appeared to have been the flawed thesis for my degree in life education!

Whenever you try to separate yourself from your emotions it's impossible to feel connected with yourself or with others. That's because you're too busy analyzing your thoughts and the related emotions. The more you resist experiencing your emotions, the longer you will stay stuck on the mental treadmill. Around and around your mind will go. And you won't take important steps to move forward towards fulfilling your big dreams. Your mind will be constantly recycling through analysis paralysis. This is what causes you to become "bogged down" in procrastination:

Dysfunctional
Resistance
Emotional
Apathy
Manufactures
Stress

You cannot consistently be moving forwards toward your goals without consistently allowing emotional responses to pass. This is because any uncertainty in your life will naturally trigger more emotional responses. When you're moving into new territory and new life experiences, these are going to be triggered often!

It takes guts to go out and get what you want from life – and the motivation and ease of doing so starts with allowing all of those emotional responses to resolve with the ease of a sneeze. The more you try to resist your current emotional state; the more people (and life) will push back at you.

Emotional balance and the feeling of ease cannot consistently be accessed from outside of yourself, so it must be generated from within. This requires re-learning a new skill, rewiring your brain to allow every emotional response to pass through you. Then you can get on with living a self-empowered life!

Many personal development experts talk about changing your state. The fastest way to change your state is by doing this one thing. This is because resistance is the very thing which keeps returning you to an undesired state of being.

Whenever you feel the intense desire to reach out to someone or to indulge in some-thing... it's a clear indicator that an emotional response has been triggered and you've ignored it or tried to make it go away.

Even though it sometimes feels uncomfortable being you, remember that every emotion is just a brief moment in time which easily passes when you allow it to.

You're not giving those thoughts your attention, you're not giving the physical discomfort your attention, you're just allowing that uncomfortable moment in time to be resolved with the ease of a sneeze.

You will only feel truly fulfilled when you start doing this one thing. To feel connected in life you need to be yourself. This means enduring the brief physical discomfort associated with your emotions. You don't need to express emotions out loud, just switch your attention to allow the brief wave of physical discomfort which is associated with them to happen. Allow emotions to be just a moment in time (which they were designed to be) and every unwanted emotion will pass within seconds.

In comparison to the separation which occurs when you try to prevent an emotion, if you simply allow an emotional response as it is triggered, you automatically relax, strengthen your connection to life and simultaneously raise your sense of selfesteem. This helps to bring you into Attraction Alignment.

How to Feel Aligned and Attractive

Can you see how one feeds off the other? Without being emotionally balanced you will always feel slightly off kilter. If we're not turning ourselves on to life and we feel apathetic (or just plain pathetic) how can we expect others to feel attracted to us? Like attracts like. If you want to attract someone and retain their attraction you need to become emotionally balanced which naturally leads to you being emotionally attractive.

This requires taking care of your own emotional fulfillment and fulfilling your own needs as a human being instead of expecting someone else to fulfil you. This means engaging in activities which fulfil you as a person. Allow emotional responses when they are triggered. Upgrade your knowledge to solve problematic areas of your life which frequently cause you to trigger. Be congruent with your values instead of altering yourself to try and fit into someone else's perspective of life.

Many of us choose to wear rose-colored glasses instead of acknowledging a red flag which indicates that our values or personal boundaries with another person are obviously conflicting. Values and boundaries can include health, lifestyle, finances and sex. While you may try to mold yourself to fit in with the other person, this usually comes with the cost of feeling like you've com-

promised yourself. Over a period of time this consistently throws you out of attraction alignment.

You need to get it correct right from the outset because resistant emotions affect attraction and libido! If you get together with someone who you are not compatible with then you will constantly be resisting them and expecting them to compromise in order for *you* to feel better.

Being attracted to another person isn't enough as there also needs to be a degree of compatibility. You won't know if you are emotionally compatible unless you are allowing all your emotional responses to resolve because this is what enables you to honestly view a situation for what it is. If you are clouded by emotion then your mind is more likely to lie, cheat and make excuses that being with SOMEONE is better than being alone. Or so you think. You're actually better off understanding how to enjoy the person you are being alone with. Yourself!

You don't feel better when you express yourself to someone, you feel better at the end of the discourse when you realize they have actually listened to you and acknowledged your point. However, as soon as you switch to being in a state of acceptance it automatically "makes you" feel better. This will also neutralize your resistance and prevent either of you from pushing a point of view.

Attraction alignment requires being present within yourself in that moment and allowing the physical discomfort of emotions instead of fighting them. This is the fastest way to feel connected with yourself and others. In that moment when you're feeling intensely present, you are immensely attractive to all people around you. Everyone starts gravitating towards you because your energy just exudes yummy and they want to be a part of it.

You're just being yourself, the delicious you that you are in the moment. You're not fighting yourself, you're just allowing whatever is to be there... Essentially, you're being really honest within yourself. And from every other person's perspective that's really attractive.

It's also a state of non-judgment because when you're experiencing yourself as you are, then you accept everyone else as they are. There isn't the sense of separation which we experience when we are trying to separate ourselves from our thoughts and emotions.

The easiest way to fall into alignment with other people is to first feel like you're in alignment with yourself. This automatically happens as soon as you stop second guessing yourself. When you're aligned with yourself, others are attracted to the sense of connection they feel when they are in your presence. Technically they can only feel this when you are aligned within *yourself*.

How to Switch Yourself Back into Attraction Alignment

Regardless of your situation and what challenges you are facing, the depth of the emotional rabbit hole you can fall into is always your choice. And whether or not you actually fall into a rabbit hole is always optional. It's always your choice to go down there. When you block an emotional response and when you try to be who you are not, you tend to land in the rabbit hole by default.

This generally happens when we start relying on another person to make us feel good. When we start thinking that it's some other person who is making us feel good, we start putting more of our attention on them instead of ourselves. We assume that it is them who is making us feel good and we become addicted to that person. We go out of alignment within ourselves as soon as we do that. And that's when the vicious loop of neediness begins.

So many times, when we are attracted to a person, we allow all the insecurities which naturally surface to plunge us into an emotional rabbit hole. Yet, our emotional balance should never be dependent on someone else because only *we* can be in charge of our emotional responses!

If you're with *that* person, be disciplined and don't let your mind keep racing off and imagining various scenarios. Think of this as a preventative method because when your mind visualizes the future too fast, it tends to trigger fear and other emotional responses as you contemplate the possibility of things going wrong. These emotional responses must be allowed (instead of analyzed) so that you can remain present and in a state of non-resistance.

When you're fighting yourself, and judging that you or someone else "should be doing this" or they "should be doing that" then in that moment you are out of alignment and turning everyone off, including yourself.

When you decide to be more disciplined and stay in the now with whomever you are with, then you will automatically enjoy more of that time together while feeling at ease. And we all want to be with people where it feels easy, right? As humans, we tend to seek the easier options in life and we also do this with our relationships.

The most important point about attraction is to stay in alignment within yourself. When you feel massive attraction for someone it's going to keep triggering weird stuff within yourself and you just have to keep being present with it. If it's emotion, allow it. If it's thoughts creating emotion, monitor the thoughts and stop them from spiraling out of control. Bring yourself back to the present by allowing the physical discomfort of that related emotion.

When you're putting your attention on what makes you feel good BY ALLOWING AND NOT FIGHTING YOURSELF (and everyone else) then you're constantly going to feel better and this will constantly intensify your depth of attraction.

As you feel better, people who are feeling better within themselves are going to be naturally drawn to you. Whereas if you're focused on being the victim or the one not fitting in then you will attract circumstances which will reflect *that* resistant state back to you. It all comes back to seeking alignment within yourself first because everything comes back to that initial point of attraction.

Align within yourself and you attract interactions with others who are aligned within themselves. The more you just place your attention on doing the things which make you feel good as a person and allowing your emotional responses as they're triggered, then the better you will feel, and you will experience better outcomes and interactions with others.

The #1 rule of attraction is to get into alignment within yourself. When you are in emotional alignment within yourself, you become "plugged into" the bigger part of yourself which radiates out and allows you to more easily feel connected with other people. You will also communicate your ideas with ease and without difficulty.

When you notice that you're fighting yourself IN ANY WAY then you need to readjust your attention and your perspective. When we decide we are happy we just switch our attention to feelings of happiness. These happy feelings are manufactured inside ourselves, by ourselves, whenever we switch our attention to allowing them to be generated!

There's a massive difference between trying to control how you feel and choosing to be in charge of how you feel. While it appears subtle, it is always your choice to *allow* yourself to feel... which then also enables attraction alignment.

Vital, Problem-Free Sex Education

The remaining piece of the puzzle is sex. There is so much confusion and conflicting messages being given about sex and how to resolve sexual dysfunctional problems. Although putting the emphasis on teaching teens how to protect themselves during sex, the sex education system in schools is sadly lacking in helpful knowledge which prepares young adults in understanding this very important arena of their lives.

It's like giving them a key, a car and a fuel voucher without teaching them the road code or giving them instructions on how to operate their vehicle. This includes how to stay in their own lane and the consequences of not understanding how to drive! NOTICE THE SIMILARITY?

Parents can only instruct their teens with what they, themselves learned. However, without explaining the complete start to end procedure required by the brain to control the sexual act, most of these well-meaning "talks" have little or no beneficial effect especially if the parents have their own sexual problems.

With that in mind, I'm devoting the next two in-depth chapters to help you gain a better understanding of the reasons sexual problems occur and some of the requirements the brain needs to ensure a mutually fulfilling sexual act. This provides real behind-the-scenes kind of insights which no-one else is sharing with you.

Remember that we're not given a manual which teaches us how to "drive" our bodies, so when things go wrong (or don't work) we have nothing to compare them with. Males tend to get their "adult" sex education from watching porn, females either from watching porn or reading romance novels. These are fairy tale scenarios based on fiction and bad examples!

For example, porn depicts women as liking it hard and fast and a constant change of position. Yet in reality these actions can prevent her from achieving orgasm and quite often will put her off wanting sex. If she wants hard and fast she will ask for it. If she doesn't ask, don't presume it as a prerequisite.

We have different sexual needs and preferences yet our sex programs all work the same way.

In romance novels, an orgasm is portrayed as a massive explosion in the Universe whereas in reality it's made up of very nice, yet sometimes subtle sensations. Of course, these sensations can be deliciously intensified by applying the correct thought and action focusing sequence which is explained in my Sex Mastery for women and Real EASY Love programs.

Although I started with a plethora of my own life issues and sexually related problems, I am now considered by many to be a world leader in solving emotional resistance and sexual dysfunctional problems.

As you will see in the statistics below, this lack of relevant knowledge leads to massive problems in our ability to relate with confidence to a partner.

Men are devastated when they can't perform sexually. Both sexes feel incomplete as a couple when they just can't seem to achieve sexual fulfilment simultaneously.

Because we're not taught a complete start-to-end procedure for sex there is a great deal of confusion involved throughout the sexual act! Sexual dysfunctions or "malfunction" problems can occur the first time a person engages in sexual activity or they can randomly occur throughout the course of a person's sexual life.

Our brain requires specific "messages" to activate the muscle programs related to sex. When the brain doesn't receive these signals - or the brain receives inconsistent signals then what I term sexual malfunction problems occur. This may include erectile dysfunction, low libido, premature ejaculation and being unable to ejaculate for men. For women, common problems include randomly losing interest during sex, lack of libido, inner vaginal dryness and problems of not being able to achieve orgasm.

The reported statistics:

> 30% of all men suffer from premature ejaculation
> 40% of men over 40 randomly or consistently lose their erection hardness
> 80% of women have problems achieving orgasm during intercourse and 20% of those women fail to achieve an orgasm at all.

It's quite evident from these statistics that there are ongoing issues for people with problems, who are not receiving answers. This includes a low success rate from so called long established experts and ineffective medical intervention.

As well as solving their initial problems, I also share the correct techniques to enhance their ability in love making. What a woman needs for emotional and physical enhancement. What a man needs to regain his confidence and ability to function confidently and successfully as a participating partner.

I supply the answers for all the problems and they are easy to understand and facilitate. There is no comparable information on the net or anywhere else which explains the foibles of sex and how-to reprogram and re-structure your brain - refer to Doctor's Testimony at the start of Part 2. This includes how to regain your ability to perform normal sex... for a normal time frame... with normally expected and enjoyable results!

It's small wonder why so many people are lacking fulfilment in their relationships. These problems often result in a low libido for either partner which is often magnified by the frustrations associated with not being able to fulfil or be fulfilled during sex.

Many men and women want to be able to satisfy their partner by being able to enjoy sex and last longer in bed. They read articles and search forums, try different positions and research foods and exercises. They take drugs or medications which have unwanted side-effects (sometimes the drugs work but they feel artificial by removing the spontaneity of sex.) Others undertake sex therapy or counselling hoping for *answers*.

They feel frustrated when nothing seems to work – and they can't figure out what they're doing wrong. Often feeling tense, anxious and nervous during sex, they are desperate to have a normal sex life, but it seems entirely out of their reach.

For example,

> Mark was a recovering drug addict and alcoholic. He had booked a session with me earlier in the year for an erectile dysfunction problem. However, he didn't show up for his initial session at our appointed time, nor did he let me know why he couldn't attend! When he contacted me about seven months later and still experiencing the same problem, I told him that this was his last chance. If he didn't show up for his next appointment, I wasn't prepared to help him. My ex-

periences with Russell taught me the importance of setting boundaries and sticking to them!

Mark insisted that he really needed my help and diligently showed up for all his sessions. He apologized for his previous behavior and said that he was a recovering drug addict and alcoholic, but he had been sober for the last six months.

On hearing his explanation, I asked how he was coping with being sober for so long. He said that he wasn't coping at all well. He explained that he had been constantly high for the past 12 years. A successful businessman with all his deals being sealed over scotch and a snort of cocaine. Whenever he started coming down, he'd take another shot of whatever was on the table.

He said that he would rarely sleep and hadn't experienced a "negative" emotion in years. Any sign of emotion was quickly numbed with alcohol or subdued with drugs and off into the stratosphere he would launch himself. There was only ever a high. Truth be told, he said he had never come down long enough to experience real emotion because he was constantly and unequivocally high.

The problem was that when he decided he ought to become sober, he had no coping strategies for dealing with life in the real world. He mentioned that he had been paying $300 once a week for a session with an esteemed psychologist. Once a week for the past three months and he *still* hadn't received any strategies to help him cope with being sober!

He had since met a girl in rehab and suddenly it was important for everything in his life to be working normally.

But without drugs he couldn't get an erection. Combined with the ignorance of not knowing how to deal with emotion he was constantly feeling anxious and nervous. Having been sober for six months he said he was constantly feeling like he needed a really strong drink!

I explained to him that I could easily solve his anxiety problem as well, so he extended the length of his initial session, so we could begin to sort out both problems.

First, I explained how the emotional response works and how to allow the physical discomfort of the emotional response to pass (instead of fighting it) whenever it's triggered. I then guided him through the process several times, so he understood how it felt mentally and physically.

Because he had come to me for an erectile dysfunction issue we used examples of *that* issue to "trigger" several emotional responses. Before his session with me it would be normal for him to focus on the actual problem and then the possible new problems. The anxiety would arise from those issues (as in the possibility of losing his new-found love) and he would continue to become more and more anxious.

Now however he was sitting dumbfounded in his seat, surprised at how relaxed and at ease he was feeling. He said that previously thinking about that issue would work him up into such a frenzy he thought he would need to have a drink.

He had previously relied on his external fixes to "fix" him whenever emotional responses were triggered. Anxiety became part and parcel of his sex problems too. He had been so used to using drugs to enhance his awareness of good feeling, he didn't realize he could enhance his sexual feelings without them.

In fact, because he was denying the physical sensations of an emotional response, the drugs had blocked him off from any awareness of reality.

Mark told me he learned more in his first hour with me than he had learned in 12 consecutive weeks of psychotherapy! Instead of wasting valuable time going around and around in explanation of his condition and analyzing his life stories, with me he was able to immediately get to the crux of the matter. I explained that allowing the physical sensations of the triggered emotional responses would enable him to feel more relaxed and at ease.

How could he feel better if he was stopping himself from experiencing everything?

He telephoned me a few days after his session to excitedly inform me that he and his girlfriend had the best sex ever and she had said that it was the best money he had ever invested! A few more sessions and he was totally set up with strategies to deal with the other challenges he faced in life.

Anxiety was part of the problem and learning how to deal with the anxiety as well as upgrading his knowledge base enabled him to restore a functioning and fulfilling life. This was without the crutch (or desire) of alcohol and drugs.

I have *so* many stories from clients who struggled to find answers in mainstream systems.

Nick used to ejaculate within seconds of penetration. He and his partner had tried everything – from a Urologist to a tantric master, the stop technique, the squeeze technique. Then he underwent sessions with two sex therapists, including treatment from a world-renowned sex therapist. Every treatment he received was really expensive and did not resolve the issue.

Then he and his partner found my website. From their first communication with me I was confident that I could solve Nick's problem – and I did. They don't have much time for sex because of their long working hours but three weeks after his initial session he reported a beautiful encounter which lasted around 40 minutes. This was at a really intense pace. He was so happy as was his girlfriend. He reported that his technique is improving every time they have sex.

David found it increasingly difficult to get an erection. Combined with premature ejaculation it was completely daunting! He had tried a popular erection drug, but it stopped working plus he was on medications for other health issues. He found my website while searching for answers online. What I said on my site made a great deal of sense, so he booked a session.

Now, David and his girlfriend live in different States, so they don't meet each other often. The second week they got together after their session with me, he reported that things were dramatically improved. He was able to easily attain erections.

The PE issue was basically non-existent. He stayed in control and could last as long as he wanted to and reported being able to regain his sexual confidence.

Jean and her husband have been married for 46 years. Although Jean loved having sex because of the emotional connection, feelings of intimacy and pleasure it brought her husband, she had given up on being able to achieve an orgasm.

At the age of 76, most experts would tell her it's impossible that she would ever overcome this dilemma. However, her husband was hopeful after reading my website and they booked a session. Six weeks later after discussing my merits at great length, they agreed what a fine thing I was doing for society. They also reported that Jean now "hits gold" nearly every time they have intercourse!

While Nick, David, and Jean's sex results look remarkable at first glance (and are definitely accomplishments to be proud of) these results aren't rocket science. The techniques they utilized can be applied by any man or woman who wants to satisfy their partner in bed and achieve a normal, happy and spontaneous sex life.

I've coached over a thousand men, women and couples of all ages and lifestyles, in varying states of health and fitness. And I've received reports of amazing results including:

> ➤ Men with erection softness to rock hard erections to ejaculation on command
> ➤ Going from ejaculating within seconds to hard and in control for over 30 mins' duration
> ➤ Unable to achieve orgasm, to orgasming on demand including during intercourse!

It's important to be able to enjoy sex and last longer in bed so you can satisfy yourself as well as your partner. I'm going to show you the common mistakes people make when trying to restore their sex life. As well as learning the new formula for restoring your sex life, it won't feel like it's hard work. Soon, you too can achieve a normal, happy, spontaneous sex life – and I'll show you how!

It's common for men and women who suffer from sex problems to be confused by all the options available. When trying to "end the problem" it can be challenging to navigate between fact and fiction.

For example, the diet and exercise myth. What about drugs and medications? Are they safe? Do they solve the problem or are they a temporary fix? Does sex therapy actually *solve* sexual dysfunctional problems?

Many men and women are excited about the possibility of being able to relax and enjoy sex. To be able to comfortably enjoy the experience of sexual intimacy so they can satisfy their partner in bed.

We've already seen that it can be easily achieved.

I shared Nick's story - changing from ejaculating within seconds of penetration to lasting around 40 minutes at what he described as a really good pace. This then made his girlfriend really happy.

And David's story too – from having problems getting hard, then ejaculating early. He changed to staying hard and in control for as long as he and his girlfriend wanted him to, all within three weeks.

Jean's result was a complete surprise to her doctor. Who would have guessed at 76 years of age she could suddenly start achieving orgasm during intercourse?

All of these things are possible! But it's impossible without the right knowledge and procedure.

When Jean and these men started out trying to solve their sex problems, they were completely overwhelmed. The guys searched on Google "how to last longer in bed" and they saw SO MANY OP-

TIONS. All of them seemed like a complete lifestyle change or something artificial which took away from the spontaneity of sex. Or it was a new and expensive type of supplement or therapy.

They all went down the path of trying to figure out how to deal with their problem. They'd try something – and it wouldn't really work so their enthusiasm would waver. They knew they had to act but would they ever be able to rectify this problem, so sex would be enjoyable, spontaneous, fun?

These are some of the mistakes men and women make when they begin trying to solve these problems. There are SO many ways to go wrong if you try to solve these problems but don't have a reliable information base to fall back on.

There are too many "experts" telling you what you want to hear, instead of what actually works.

Here are the 3 biggest myths that I see many men and women fall victim to – and I can help you avoid them:

1. "I Can Take This Drug and My Problem Will Go Away" Myth

I've had feedback from hundreds of men (who had visited men's clinics, urologists, and their doctors), that erectile dysfunction and premature ejaculation drugs and medications don't work. Or they initially worked and then they appeared to stop working. Or that they were painful, or artificial, or that the side effects were horrendous and lasted for days.

And that as soon as they stopped using the medications their problem returned in full – sometimes worse than before. On top of these issues the generic "safe" brands can cost $15 each time you have sex!

They realized that drugs and medications don't solve the problem (and would NEVER solve the problem). Then they made a breakthrough and discovered a way to last longer so they could satisfy their partner in bed. A unique method that didn't get short term results but enabled them to have consistently great sex.

2. The "Sex Therapy and Counselling" Myth

Surely a sex therapist would teach you what you need to know about lasting longer, right?

Wrong. Most sex therapists and counselors just deal with the psychological factors which can affect your sex life including work-related stress and anxiety, sexual performance anxiety, marital or relationship problems, depression, feelings of guilt and the effects of past sexual trauma. But they do not solve the actual reason why this started in the beginning.

As I experienced myself, while it was helpful to talk about these things, it doesn't teach you how to solve your sexual dysfunction problem. A sex therapist may also teach you about the sexual response cycle and the elements of sexual stimulation. Drugs are commonly recommended by sex therapists.

Other recommendations from sex therapists include: the squeeze technique, the stop-start technique, testosterone therapy, sprays or topical creams, Kegel exercises, penis devices, herbs, yoga, pelvic muscle exercises, sensate focus exercises, non-sexual touching techniques. Including positively communicating your wants and desires and learning to relax.

Therapists offer counseling, medications or techniques which only treat the symptoms. This means that you're still left wondering if your actual problem's going to be solved or not.

They do not address the "root cause" if you will excuse the pun!

3. The "Diet and Exercise Will Help Me Last Longer" Myth

What about all the internet sites which state: "if you avoid these foods" or "if you eat these foods" or "exercise your sex muscles" you'll be able to enjoy sex, last longer and satisfy your partner in bed? If so many people promise this, it has to be true, right?

Wrong. The truth is that MANY men and women eat well, exercise regularly (including Kegel exercises) and are in overall good shape. They think their sex life should be going well but it isn't.

They would start sex with the right frame of mind then a little nugget of doubt intervenes. This would then snowball into a cascade of random thoughts including trying not to think about losing the erection, losing control or not being able to achieve an orgasm.

These men figured there wasn't anything physically wrong because they would sometimes get an erection or last longer when masturbating or have sex with a partner without any problems. They knew it must be something else but couldn't figure it out. They wanted to stop feeling tense and anxious during sex and were hopeful for an answer.

It IS important to check with a doctor to ensure any underlying health issues or medical conditions are being addressed.

In my experience, in most cases you can forget the usual sex advice. This advice tells you, you need to exercise, take drugs or endure months of therapy to be able to enjoy sex, last longer and satisfy your partner in bed. It's not necessary! Instead, with advanced knowledge and a few precise "tweaks" to your current procedure while having foreplay or intercourse, you can take control of your body and achieve a consistently great sex life!

Your brain needs to receive and transmit relevant messages (signals) to be able to get hard, stay hard, control ejaculation and orgasm whenever you want to. You can change how your brain reacts to the messages you give it by upgrading the information that you are storing in your brain.

This is why aligning your thoughts and actions are so important.

My unique Sex Mastery and Real EASY Love programs will help men and women who suffer from sex problems gain the skills and confidence to have a spontaneous, normal and happy sex life. These programs will also help older teens *prevent* these common sexual malfunction problems from occurring. With this knowledge, everyone can relax, enjoy sex and satisfy their partner in bed without feeling like it's doomed to failure!

Understanding Male and Female Sex Problems

I spoke about the Switching Technique in an earlier chapter. The switching technique is a method used to control the natural switching which occurs between your conscious and subconscious minds. Just like a computer, your conscious mind "switches" to access the data and programs stored in your subconscious mind. Switching also naturally occurs when you switch your attention from a thought to an action or from one task to another.

This switching becomes vitally important during sex.

It's normal for your mind to lose focus. But during sex you need to re-organize your thoughts to ensure you keep the correct focus sequence and activate the correct muscle programs attached to that or those thoughts.

Your conscious mind can only focus on one thing at a time and the destination of that focus dictates which muscle programs are activated in your brain. You must literally center your focus onto the correct subject matter - as thinking of something else or thinking of a previous subject will divert your attention and cause mental chaos.

A functioning sexual union between a male and a female is determined by two factors:

How long it takes for *her* to finish orgasming
How long it takes for *him* to ejaculate

Now remember that a woman can take up to TWENTY minutes to achieve her desired amount of orgasms for example; 5. Whereas a man takes ONE minute to ejaculate once he's initiated the ejaculation program. So, on that premise, a male must keep sexually active for 20 minutes while she orgasms, *then* he ejaculates.

Their efforts need to be synchronized so they are on the same "playing field."

The problems which are usually encountered for a female are that she doesn't get turned on, doesn't stay turned on, has difficulty achieving orgasm, or can't orgasm at all.

This may be due to a problem with her male, he can't get a hard on, he will lose hardness, he will ejaculate early, or he won't ejaculate at all. This means she doesn't reach her allotment before he ejaculates, or he can't get a hard on.

If this is the case, she must manipulate him to get the desired result. This is fully explained in my Sex Mastery and Real EASY Love programs which ultimately have the capacity to solve any sexual problem for both men, women and couples.

For a male, erectile dysfunction and premature ejaculation are similar problems caused by a different approach from the brain for each problem. My system differentiates between the two and provides a lasting remedy to solve both problems and allows the sufferer to overcome either if they arise.

If the male is suffering from erectile dysfunction I provide the solution for him to attain an erection. This solution enables him to attain an erection then maintain it for the duration of the act including foreplay, penetration and intercourse. This remedy will solve most of the immediate problems, however he can supplement further knowledge from my advanced programs.

The appropriate programs also cover premature ejaculation. With this advanced knowledge, he will find an easy to follow procedure which instantly deals with his malfunction. This will restore his confidence, so he can enjoy a lovemaking session without any untimely interruption.

Whenever a male loses his erection or loses ejaculation control it is a cause for concern. This disruption will totally end any hope of him fulfilling his sexual role. He will be distracted and thinking about the overwhelming circumstances and then consequently losing control of his erection hardness or ejaculate due to this pressure. With a malfunctioning penis, he can't participate with (her) any further and she has barely started her pleasure time!

My programs supply all the answers to rectify these problems.

If he ejaculates early, it is the beginning of the initial problem. It is basically selfishness even though it is usually unintentional and could be considered a loss of self-control. REMEMBER it only takes one minute for a male to ejaculate (once he initiates the ejaculation program) whereby if he chooses the wrong moment, it ends up being a disaster because she has been short changed in sexual participation time!

It is common for men with any of these problems to go from one extreme to the other as they worry about how their penis is going to perform.

Can't get a hard, ED, PE and can't ejaculate all stem from the same erotic zone but for different reasons. Males can transition through any variation of the above. The answers to all these problems are presented in my Sex Mastery: Hard and in Control program for males, so he doesn't have any confusion later!

The answers to both male *and* female problems are fully explained in my Real EASY Love programs. I'll explain some more insights for both sexes in this chapter.

Firstly, I need to explain the female perspective. Her amount of arousal is also the measurement of how much pleasure she feels. If she is under aroused she may experience losing interest and being unable to orgasm. However, when she's aroused and actively participating, it feels good, she's emotionally engaging with her partner and her sensations feel intense to the point where she can easily achieve an orgasm.

When a woman has difficulty achieving orgasms she has become distracted which makes her lose awareness of any feeling of arousal.

It may be too much time spent doing (or thinking) other things and not enough emphasis on trying to intensify her sensations while attempting to reach "the turned-on zone." With a failing structure to perform good sex (and her declining desire for sex) her partner is going through the motions and she has stopped participating!

REMEMBER her mind can wander and switch off her libido in less than a minute which ends up being a disaster because both of you have been shortchanged in sexual participation time!

Think of sex as a game of strategy which you're playing! Once you understand the procedure, boundaries and limitations, the game of sex will become much more relaxing, enjoyable and fun.

Sexual control requires balancing
The Sexual Trifecta:

1. Sexually arousing thoughts
2. Sexually arousing feelings (sensations)
3. Sexually arousing actions

This could also be called your sexual focus. Your brain analyzes these "messages" then moves you along the arousal scale accordingly.

For both sexes, sexual focus is vitally important, so both partners need to input an equal amount of participation. Without the correct balance, your brain will become confused or distracted and this is the beginning of ALL problems. You must interrupt negative thoughts during sex before they snowball and cause loss of control in either partner.

This is why it's so important to solve the emotional reaction when it's triggered!

The process for balancing the sexual focus is more complex for males: Generally, foreplay requires more focus on his partner and attending to the physical actions of giving his partner oral or manual stimulation.

She would appreciate more attention on making foreplay an awesome experience for herself. This distraction can divert too much attention onto her so the "act" becomes lopsided.

Allowing yourself to worry about what might happen next during sex is the most common cause of sexual performance anxiety and related sex problems. This anxiety needs to be solved when it's triggered otherwise you won't be able to think clearly and this leads to mistakes.

Now let me be clear: Worrying about possible problems *causes* anxiety. Anxiety isn't the only thing causing sex problems, it's an *effect* of having this problem. The answers contained within my Sex Mastery and Real EASY programs will resolve sexual anxiety problems by providing the complete start to end procedure that your brain requires for sex

When you have this knowledge, you will naturally regain confidence in yourself and in your ability to fulfil and be fulfilled sexually. In the meantime, you need to allow an emotional response to pass if it's triggered. When you just try to stop feeling anxious it puts you in a brain freeze: you still won't be able to think clearly because you're still focusing on the *thoughts about the problem.*

For the most part, anxiety is a PHYSICAL response caused by over thinking and negative thoughts – it's not the actual thoughts themselves. By briefly switching your attention to allow the PHYSICAL DISCOMFORT of the emotional response you will prevent negative thoughts about sex from snowballing. This works like a reset button because your conscious mind can only focus on one thing at a time.

Instead of fighting it, consciously allow the PHYSICAL discomfort of an emotional response to happen if it's triggered: (Increased heart rate! Muscle tension! Bated breath!) Physically this feels intense and uncomfortable. But as soon as you switch your attention to allow that moment of discomfort - it's gone! (Like a sneeze.)

This immediately interrupts a negative thought pattern, so you can think clearly. You can then refocus your attention for hard and in control or to easily achieve orgasms.

The way you approach solving sex problems is the same way you approach solving the other problems in your life:

> ➤ Stop fighting the physical discomfort of the anxiety and ALWAYS allow the brief associated discomfort related to the emotional response. This includes when an emotional response is triggered during the sexual act as well as when they are randomly triggered when thinking about your sex problems.

> ➤ Obtain the complete start to end procedure for sex that your brain requires so you can confidently engage in the sexual act for the mutual fulfilment of both partners.

> ➤ Follow through with the complete strategy laid out and don't shortcut the system. Don't allow your mind to lie, cheat and make excuses!

You can do it!

Sex is such an important component of a mutually fulfilling relationship. For a male, it cements his emotional connection with his partner and makes him feel more of a man. For a female, it enhances her feeling of connection with her partner and increases her feelings of trust.

A man without sex is like a fish without water and a woman without an emotional connection can feel as remote as the desert sands. Can you see why it's so important to solve these problems?

Men generally don't go through the female equivalent of menopause. This means most men retain an active sex drive well into their eighties. Can you imagine how depressing it is for a male when his partner stops wanting sex in her fifties?

Any aversion to sex a man has is usually related to his own sexual dysfunction problem. This happened in my own relationship with Russell, sometimes a man's sexual dysfunction is caused by his partner's indifference and non-participation in sex.

When a woman displays a lack of interest in sex (if it's not health related) it's generally for one of these reasons:

> ➤ She has problems achieving orgasm or can't orgasm at all
> ➤ Her partner has an ongoing weak erection, early ejaculation or delayed ejaculation issue
> ➤ She doesn't fully trust him yet
> ➤ She doesn't enjoy her partner's technique

> ➤ She is experiencing emotional resistance towards him

When she can't achieve orgasm or it's a huge mission to achieve orgasm she may lose interest in sex. A woman requires emotional fulfilment for sex to be enjoyable and a portion of this is required from her partner during sex. This means that even if she's switching to allow her own emotional responses when they're triggered due to her own issue, she can still experience emotional disconnection from her partner if he isn't aligned with her.

If her partner is constantly worrying about his ability to get an erection, or worrying about losing his erection, or worrying about ejaculating early, or worrying about not being able to ejaculate... then at those times she will sense NO emotional connection with him. This will distract her mind and create new problems.

Usually women are so in tune with their partners they can sense when he's not enjoying himself. This will directly affect her own ability to enjoy sex.

These are the most common sexual problems and prevalent causes (non-medically related):

Performance anxiety for the most part isn't the initial cause of sex problems, it's an effect of having a problem. Solve the sex problem and you'll solve most of the sexual anxiety problem. As previously stated, anxiety is part of the emotional response program in your brain and can be immediately cleared with my "Ease of a Sneeze" technique.

Generally, emotional problems present themselves when knowledge and skills are lacking in any area.

Premature ejaculation is problematic during sex because it disrupts the flow of energy which was initially present. By ejaculating first, the male has put the handbrake on the proceedings and prevented the other partner from any further participation. This one-sided result can cause anxiety, anger and frustration for the person who did not complete the act.

He needs a completely new strategy to overcome this anomaly, so he can take into consideration the needs of his partner. This apparent lack of concern is the reason for many relationship breakups. It doesn't have to be this way. With the correct information, he can rid himself of this problem efficiently and quickly.

Erectile dysfunction is a condition from which the male will lose his hard. This is because his concentration has tended to wander from its primary focus. The proven strategy I supply gives the male the exact mental coordinates to complete his part of the act. This in turn, will provide an uninterrupted passage from start to finish for both partners during the sexual act. Accidental "glitches" will be a thing of the past.

Can't ejaculate is a "mental blockage" causing a "physical blockage!" This blockage is easily rectified with an exact mental procedure. This is an easy to cure problem identifying a "wrong turn" as the culprit. My programs can make short work of this problem.

Unable to achieve orgasm typically stems from a brain * vagina mismatch. Once the wheel alignment has been corrected there will be no steering wobbles. Typically, the woman will be able to orgasm normally after this correction. With the advanced Real EASY Love program, I provide additional modules which guide the woman through any disruptions and allow her to embellish the relationship with advanced knowledge.

Low libido is often caused by a combination of the above conditions or a partner's unsatisfactory technique. This is also rectified by the program mentioned above which includes the initial reason for low libido as well as upskilling a partner's technique. This applies to both male and female. This will negate the need for verbal instructions to his penis asking, "Come on, get hard!" A penis has a head with no brain, does that explain things? It doesn't work. Get the instant answers now!

Now this isn't something which is shared by doctors or other medical professionals. It's not taught at universities, you wouldn't learn it from a sex therapist or any other "expert" in the realm of resolving sexual dysfunction problems.

This knowledge is unique to me, and the Tohunga who initially taught me.

Using this unique Switching Technique methodology I've helped over a thousand men, women and couples globally to understand the order in which their emotional and sexual programs need to operate in order for them to be able to resurrect a fulfilling sex life.

The majority of my clients report fantastic success. Instead of wondering if their problem was ever going to be solved, from their first session with me they started receiving the answers they had spent so long searching for. My methods are even endorsed by medical specialists who have undergone remedial sessions with me.

> Brian is a medical specialist who developed erectile dysfunction after prostate surgery. He travelled the world to attend medical conferences in the hope of solving his erectile dysfunction problem. In his own words, "No medical specialists are able to provide a permanent solution for erectile dysfunction, they have no idea how to solve it."
>
> A couple of weeks after his session with me he excitedly called me to say, "I am amazed at how well this technique works! Some-

times I lose focus and start losing the erection – but now I know how to immediately get it back!"

And Sam, another medical specialist who inadvertently termed the concept of my Sex Mastery "Hard AND in Control!" program for men when he reported these results:

"I couldn't believe it! After a lifetime of ejaculating within a minute (and for the past 5 years losing my erection hardness within one minute as well) I was able to stay HARD AND IN CONTROL for over 10 minutes – just 4 days after my session with Jacqui – and the next time I had sex! It's blown my mind!"

In 2014, I was audited by the New Zealand Advertising Standards Authority and passed with flying colors when I provided this letter of recommendation from another leading medical specialist:

Re: Ms Jacqueline Olliver

"I am a medical specialist in the area of cancer medicine. She gives advice in the difficult area of sexual function problems, an area giving concern to many cancer patients. I am familiar with the teaching of Ms Olliver and am happy to recommend her treatment method."

You cannot truly feel complete as an adult human until sexual dysfunctions have been resolved. There are several anomalies between how sex is portrayed in romance novels, porn, TV and the movies and the reality of how your brain needs to trigger the right programs. Therefore, there is a distinct difference between the sex education we have received and the sex education we actually require to be able to sexually function properly as a human being.

> *"I have a dream, and in that dream, I see the confidence which men and women portray to the external world mirrored behind their bedroom door.*
>
> *In that dream, these men and women aren't inwardly faltering at the thought of having sex... They don't alienate their partner with an endless stream of excuses as to why they can't (or don't want to) have sex.*
>
> *They don't retire to bed early pretending they are too tired or that they have a headache, or are feeling "hormonal" or not in the mood. They don't dread the moment their partner throws back the covers and eases into bed immediately reaching towards them...*
>
> *I have a dream and in that dream men and women don't live within a sphere of constant tension, diminishing feelings of self-worth, or doubt their ability to fully function in a relationship. They never worry that their partner will leave them because they don't feel sexually fulfilled.*
>
> *They don't regularly experience a low libido because of their sexual empathy for their partner, or suffer from a phobia of being sexually inadequate. They don't constantly feel humiliated, embarrassed or disappointed before, during or after sex.*

There is no fear of them avoiding sex because of any impending failures. They don't avoid sex or pretend that they don't want it just, so they don't feel like a failure. They don't feel burdened by guilt or feel powerless to be able to change their situation, fearing they will be stuck with this handicap forever.

Whether they are single or in a relationship, they don't go to bed at night feeling inadequate, unlovable or insecure. They are not left wondering if they will ever be able to function as a human being and feel totally fulfilled in this important area of their life.

I have a dream, and in this dream men and women understand that their previous attempts at sex failed not because of some defect within themselves or their partner but because they were simply missing some vital knowledge.

I have a dream, and in that dream, men and women have this new knowledge and are fearless when entering new relationships knowing they have the skills to fulfil a partner sexually. With this knowledge, they boldly reignite a current relationship, are courageous in their desire to move forwards together and are convinced by their newfound abilities to fulfil and be fulfilled.

I have a dream and in that dream all men and women understand the "Switching Technique" and realize the order in which their sexual programs need to work. They are confident in their ability to provide a fulfilling emotional as well as sexual connection for themselves and their partner.

In my dream, sex is mutually desired by both partners where there is a mutual sharing of each other's happiness and joyful participation is the norm.

In my dream, men and women don't believe that sex is a chore or an obligation – an act of duty to keep the peace or something they have to endure in a relationship... Instead it has become a wondrous game of shared intimacy and connection with passion which they gladly initiate, desire and enjoy.

In my dream, I see the confidence which men and women portray to the external world, mirrored behind their bedroom door."

~ Jacqui Olliver

Abstinence Vs Real-Life Sex Education (The Sex ED Every Teen Wants, Needs)

Young adults all over the world are screaming out for a relevant sex education which explains the mental mechanics of sex so they can participate as a fully functioning human being.

Due to the embarrassment of having to discover the mechanics of sex in secrecy behind closed doors, sexual acts amongst young people are often performed in haste. This frequently leads to unplanned pregnancies and will cause sexual dysfunctional problems amongst both men and women who later become parents. This problem will plague them for many years.

If you are a parent, you need to take a step back and look at the bigger picture!

Abstinence means no sex. However, the way your teen's minds work is if they constantly try not to think about sex because it is prohibited, then they will predominantly do it anyway. The more they try not to think about it, the more their mind is consumed with those thoughts about wanting to have sex. Add their hormonal response to the mix and the problem is elevated.

This is a major factor contributing to sexual abuse in all areas of life around the globe. Young adult males are constantly told not to think about how horny they're feeling. Combined with blocking emotional responses when they are triggered, this will compound their feelings of frustration and their sexual appetites.

I have previously discussed the effects of blocking the physical discomfort of an emotional response: mental confusion, being unable to think clearly, making poor choices and bad decisions which we later regret!

The more these young men try not to feel sexually aroused, the more emotional responses are triggered and the more sexually aware they become. This works the same way for young women as well.

If teens are going to have sex irrespective of what they are told NOT to do, wouldn't you prefer them to be properly prepared and informed? This would involve the entire sexual act without any of the above mentioned dysfunctional problems. This is entirely achievable with my start to finish sex strategy programs. I would guide them completely through the mental and physical aspects, leaving no area of doubt in their mind. This sexual journey would set them up for life and rid them of promiscuity, doubt and uncertainty. There would be NO TRIAL AND ERROR!

Considering most teens have no real knowledge or understanding of how their sexual programs work, in their haste to complete sex before being discovered by adults, they miss out on the true beauty and depth of connection the act could provide to both partners.

If they encounter problems such as ejaculating early, losing erection hardness or being unable to achieve orgasm, these teens frequently become "promiscuous" and seek out casual sexual encounters. This is to gain more experience in the hope of understanding their "malfunction" problems. They are simply seeking to understand how their body works so they can become more competent as a sexually functioning human being.

We all try to improve our ability to the point we feel confident within ourselves and confident of our improved capabilities. Other teens who experience sexual dysfunction will avoid intimacy and relationships and unwillingly be alone and promiscuous.

Lack of real knowledge and understanding of the sexual act can contribute to a lack of confidence and low self-esteem. Combined with a growing sense of emotional disconnection caused from habitually blocking emotional responses when they're triggered, many teens constantly seek sexual gratification by masturbation or consenting sex to get their "feeling fix". Those who aren't given consent sometimes "take it" because of their overwhelming desire to feel "fixed."

Sex is a special part of life and needs to be communicated in a special manner. Adults have difficulty when explaining sex because they themselves have no idea of the correct procedure when broken down step-by-step. And if they themselves suffer from sex problems, what relevant and beneficial knowledge could they pass on to the future generation?

Various surveys of young adults globally are showing that teens want sex education to be more "direct, RELEVANT and comprehensive".

That requirement hasn't changed. I remember when I was a teen at school, eagerly waiting for sex education so I could finally learn how to feel fulfilled sexually. I couldn't believe it when we were only taught how NOT to get pregnant (or the boys told how NOT to get a girl pregnant), how NOT to catch STD's and then we were given a couple of condoms each... just in case. Apparently, that was the preferred and advanced Sex Education program!

What message is that communicating? It's a contradiction to distribute condoms then say, "Have NO sex, but these will prevent the STD's and pregnancy because we know you're probably going to have sex anyway." Abstinence sex education is more ambiguous and confusing than helpful - and certainly doesn't provide the answers and remedies which so many teens are looking for!

I remember that I myself kept waiting and hoping... surely, they're going to teach us relevant skills to use?? But no further knowledge about the essential skills of sexual engagement was forthcoming.

Without that detailed "how to" education which explains the mental and physical integration concerning sex, teens are going to experiment to find out what does and doesn't work. After all, who wants to lose the opportunity of being in a long-term relationship with someone because of a failure over sex? Teens are desperate to understand how it all works so they can mentally prepare for a relationship which is fulfilling on all levels.

Sex education is taught about safety but not about technique and quality! The end result of this is, younger people will naturally experiment to try and get a better understanding of sex! Invariably bad experiences, bad technique and bad habits all contribute to a total lack of skills which then lead the participants into a realm of uncertainty from which they usually never return.

Older teens are expecting that "relevant and comprehensive" sex education will set them up for success as an adult. But that will never eventuate because the programs that are currently taught are ineffective. This results in a huge percentage of adults (statistically over 30%) with sexual dysfunction problems. I'm on a mission to rectify this situation because the lack of relevant knowledge promotes massive problems involving their ability to relate physically and mentally with confidence to a partner.

Adults have a phobia concerning talking about sex to minors. This means the minors grow up into adults with phobias because they have no understanding about what is involved in the intricacies of sex. This information was never discussed.

Conversely,

When a male teen gains confidence by understanding the procedure required to confidently complete a sexual act, it makes him feel empowered as a man. Combined with understanding the necessary steps to fulfil himself and his partner (by allowing emotional responses to resolve with the ease of a sneeze and to understand attraction alignment) he loses the desire to be sexually promiscuous or to "prove" his sexual prowess to other young men.

No longer a boy who needs to "score" or talk about his heroism in the locker room, he becomes a self-assured and self-aware teen exuding confidence. Now that he knows how to sexually integrate with a partner, he has his mind firmly fixed on the future. Rather than being promiscuous, this knowledge helps him grow as a person, to become a better man and make better choices.

When a female teen also enjoys this skill, she feels good about herself and her ability to interact with others. She is then more likely to abstain from sex and wait for the right opportunity. She is more likely to wait until she is older and has developed a more secure and meaningful relationship with her eye on the future.

These results are best achieved with a real-life sex education as provided in my Sex Mastery and Real EASY programs for men and women. These programs which solve common sex problems will also prevent them from happening in the beginning!

The programs combine knowledge and skills to enhance a person's self-confidence and self-esteem. This will set your teen up for success and fulfilment in this very important area of their life.

In Summary

I believe there is an answer for every problem and that every person has the capacity to, or has already figured out one or more components of the complex "Life" puzzle. Having unequivocally solved my own problems, my most important contribution is to provide the missing answer to others. This includes information to solve sex problems, restore full emotional balance and understand attraction alignment to enrich the person as a whole.

My original vision was to disclose a method which would "do this one thing and change your life forever." I feel that I have revealed answers to negate emotional repression which causes so many problems in relationships. I state that to amplify these claims including sexual malfunctions, requires more data than is allowable in this book so I created programs which are accessible on my website www.EndTheProblem.com

My Sex Mastery and Real EASY Love programs are designed to provide answers on all aspects of intimacy. Sex Mastery is aimed at rectifying all sexual dysfunctions while Real Easy Love is designed to fully explain emotional balance, attraction alignment and sexual function. This allows you to accomplish everything you need to have a successful, happy and loving relationship with yourself and others.

Sex Mastery: Hard AND in Control! (men)
https://endtheproblem.com/male

Sex Mastery: Easily Achieve Orgasms! (women)
https://endtheproblem.com/female

Real EASY Love (for men and women)
https://endtheproblem.com/easy

Sign up for Jacqui's 5 Crucial Rules of Sex
https://endtheproblem.com/rules

I learned the hard way and wasted many of my junior years in ignorance of these paramount, vital and necessary life skills. Don't let you or your loved ones suffer due to ignorance too!

Index

ABOUT THE AUTHOR

Jacqui Olliver

Jacqui Olliver had an extraordinary start to life. Plagued by personal problems she stumbled through life mystified by the complexity of unrequited love. Right from childhood she encountered insurmountable problems. She couldn't fit into the norm. Her self-doubt blossomed into a mission. Solve the answer of how love is generated. Understand the essence of a relationship. Feel like she belonged somewhere. So, upon reaching adulthood she undertook different paths to try and expand her knowledge base. She learned different skills with her enquiring mind. By a huge fluke of luck, she stumbled onto the ultimate answer.

This answer unraveled all of her doubts in life and pushed her into the spotlight. Now she had a beacon of hope for herself and all the people in similar circumstances whom she had made a pledge to help. She took monstrous strides in her development (gaining additional qualification via Cognitive Behavioral Therapy) exceeded all her expectations and changed from a national identity into an internationally renowned adviser and mentor on the above subjects. Initially dealing with national clients, she expanded her audience internationally.

Jacqui now thrills audiences globally with her candid observations on life and how to overcome the common stumbling blocks which prevent people from experiencing a sense of peace and well-being. Her thought-provoking and witty sentiments capture the essence of life's most commonly occurring problems to which she provides unparalleled answers.

A Note from the Author:

I'm glad this book called your attention, and I'd be honored to know that it's helping you move forward in a more happy and balanced state from this point on. I want you to know that you are worthy and loved, and I believe in you. Various ways to connect with me are available below.

It's my intention to help as many people as I can with my breakthrough methods. If you could take a few minutes to rate this book on Amazon, I would most appreciate it. I've created a page on my website where you can also easily request libraries and bookstores to stock it.

Special discounts and licensing options are available on quantity purchases by libraries, schools, associations and corporations.

Links throughout this book and ALL social media links as well as contact details for Jacqui can be found here: https://endtheproblem.com/doing

Buy this book at your favorite online retailer: https://endtheproblem.com/buy

Ask Libraries to stock this book: (Doing This One Thing Will Change MANY Lives Forever!) https://endtheproblem.com/library

Join Jacqui's Real EASY Love movement and community on Facebook. https://facebook.com/groups/RealEasyLove/

For speaking engagements, personal consultations and other consulting requirements please contact Jacqui via her website: https://endtheproblem.com

Printed in Poland
by Amazon Fulfillment
Poland Sp. z o.o., Wrocław